COMPUTER NETWORKS AND DESIGN

A. Deepa
Associate Professor,
Dept of CSE, Sathyabama Institute
of Science and Technology

M.K. Dharani
Assistant Professor,
Dept of CSE, Sathyabama Institute
of Science and Technology

T. Anitha
Assistant Professor,
Dept of CSE, Sathyabama Institute
of Science and Technology

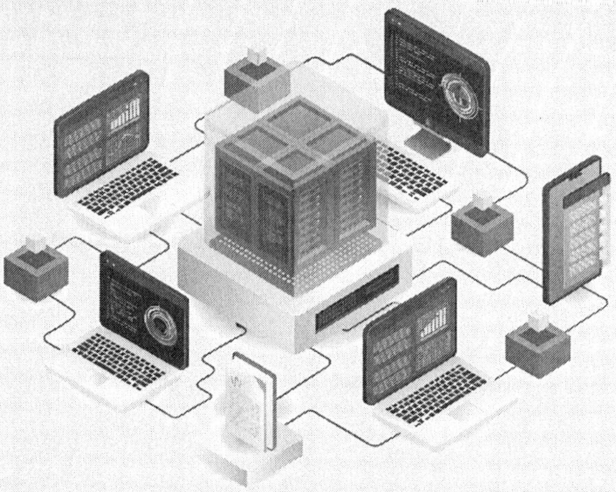

KHANNA BOOK PUBLISHING CO. (P) Ltd.
4C/4344, Ansari Road, Darya Ganj,
New Delhi, India

Sathyabama Institute of Science and Technology
Jeppiaar Nagar, Rajiv Gandhi Salai,
Chennai, Tamilnadu, India

ISBN: 978-93-55385-31-4

COMPUTER NETWORKS AND DESIGN

by **A. Deepa; M.K. Dharani; T. Anitha**

First Edition: 2026

To view complete list of books, please scan the QR Code:

Published by:
Khanna Book Publishing Co. (P) Ltd.
CIN: U22110DL1998PTC095547

Visit us at: www.khannabooks.com
Write us at: contact@khannabooks.com

Printed in Bharat.

Preface

In an era where network infrastructures form the backbone of modern enterprises, understanding the principles of network design and implementation is crucial. This book aims to provide a comprehensive guide to network design methodologies, emerging technologies, and practical implementations for businesses of all sizes.

Unit 1 introduces fundamental design principles, covering requirement analysis, existing network evaluation, and the process of transitioning from preliminary to final network designs. It also delves into the deployment, monitoring, and maintenance of networks, emphasizing the importance of modular and hierarchical design strategies for scalability and efficiency.

Unit II explores underlying LAN concepts, offering insights into LAN connectivity for small businesses, integration techniques, and technologies such as Ethernet, Token-Ring, ATM LAN emulation, and inter-LAN switching. It also provides guidance on building networks that effectively connect with mainframes.

Unit III discusses the increasing reliance on secure, remote communication, by focussing on VPNs, Intranets, and Extranets. Topics include virtual network management, VPNs tailored for small businesses, secure remote access, IPSec VPNs, and the integration of data centers with corporate intranets. Additionally, it examines the implementation and support of extranets for extended business collaboration.

Unit IV introduces networking tools and techniques essential for designing and optimizing modern networks. It discusses simulation methods for multimedia networks, remote bridge and router delay analysis, and network baselining as an effective planning tool.

Unit V covers emerging trends in data communications As technology continues to evolve, staying ahead of advancements is vital. The topics include xDSL technology, cable modem preparation, and the integration of voice and video over LANs. It also delves into cutting-edge applications such as Internet-based voice communication, IP PBX telephony networks, fax over IP, and videoconferencing over IP networks.

This book is designed to be an invaluable resource for students, network professionals, and IT managers seeking to enhance their understanding of modern networking principles and technologies. Through structured modules and practical insights, it aims to bridge the gap between theoretical concepts and real-world applications, fostering a deeper comprehension of network design and implementation.

We hope that this book serves as a valuable reference in your journey toward mastering network design and implementation.

Contents

1

UNIT Fundamentals of Network Design

RATIONALE

This unit covers network design principles, guiding learners through the process of determining requirements, analyzing existing networks, and creating preliminary and final designs. It emphasizes modular and hierarchical network design for scalability and efficiency. It explores deployment, monitoring, maintenance, and redesigning to ensure optimal performance. The importance of design documentation is highlighted to support long-term network management and troubleshooting, equipping learners with essential skills for building and sustaining robust network infrastructures.

OUTCOMES

Understand the principles of networks:

- **Comprehensive Network Design Understanding**: Learners will gain in-depth knowledge of network design principles, including requirement analysis, modular and hierarchical design, documentation, and deployment strategies, ensuring they can create scalable, efficient, and secure network architectures.
- **Practical Implementation and Maintenance Skills**: Learners will develop the ability to analyze existing networks, prepare preliminary and final designs, deploy networks, and implement ongoing monitoring, redesign, and maintenance strategies to optimize network performance and reliability.

1.1 COMPUTER NETWORK

A Computer Network (CN) is a collection of various computing devices that can share data.

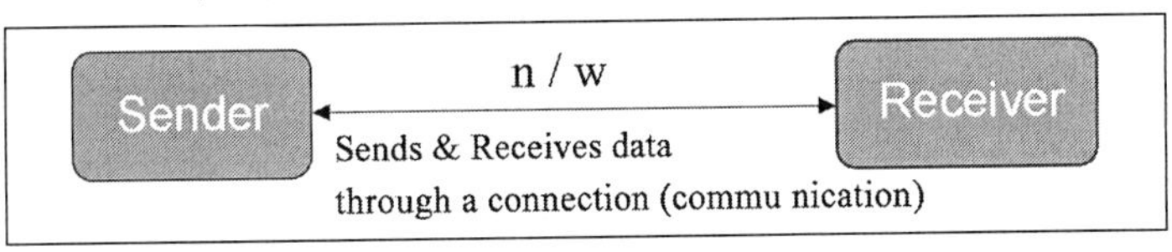

Fig. 1.1

The data sent by the sender is received by the receiver and the data is understood by the receiver. This is achieved by proper communication, i.e. connection with proper protocol.

- **Node:** Devices that are connected to a network. E.g. Computer, server, printer, router, switches.
- **Client:** Program that runs on a local machine requesting service from a server.
- **Server:** Program that runs on a remote machine providing services to the client.

The client and server can be in different locations, but they can still communicate. This is achieved through computer networks.

- **Protocol:** It is a set of rules and standards through which the transmission of data is achieved over a network.
- **Topology:** Physical and logical arrangements of nodes on a network.
- E.g. Star, mesh, bus, ring, tree
- **IP address:** A unique numerical identifier that is assigned to every device on a network.
- **Domain Name System (DNS):** It is a protocol that is used to translate human-readable domain names into IP addresses that computers can understand.
- **Firewall:** Security device that is used to monitor and control incoming and outgoing network traffic.

1.1.1 Applications of CN

Resource sharing	Can share hardware devices.
Communication	Emails, broadcasts
Home application	User-user communication, entertainment, e-commerce.
Business application	Companies working through online mode.
Social media	Facebook, Twitter, etc.
Access to remote information	Online browsing, booking train tickets, flight tickets.
Cloud computing	Store & access data and applications from a remote server.
Virtualization	Multiple virtual machines can run on a single physical machine improving resource utilization & reducing cost.
Online Education	Virtual classrooms, distance education, e-courses & classes.
Remote working	Working online (working from home)
E-Commerce	Global market for online trading.
Telemedicine	E-doctors, e-consultation, remote medical consultation & diagnosis.
Realtime collaboration	Allows global companies to get together to work on projects.

1.1.2 Advantages of CN

- Central storage of data
- Connectivity
- Fast problem-solving
- Reliability
- Flexibility
- Security through authorization
- Storage capacity

1.1.3 Disadvantages of CN

- Expensive (requires network devices)
- Virus & Malware
- Management requires a skilled person
- Loss of information
- Hacking

1.1.4 First Network

ARPANET - **A**dvanced **R**esearch **P**rojects **A**gency **NET**work

1.1.5 Characteristics of Computer Network

- Resource sharing
- Communication Speed
- Backup
- Scalability
- Reliability
- Software Hardware Sharing
- Security

Network Devices

HUB	Joins multiple devices on the same LAN
Switch	Forwards data to the destination
Bridge	Connection between 2 LANs
Gateway	Connects different networks
Modem	Modulates & demodulates signals
Router	Directs data from one network to another
Repeater	Strengthens the signal & retransmits

Network Types

1. PAN – Personal Area Network

- Connects personal devices such as a smartphone, laptop, wireless headphones, and smartwatch.
- It links personal electronic devices within a single user's workspace.
- It typically does not connect different PANs and is usually centered around one main device.
- The range is very short, typically less than 10 meters (usually within a home).
- It is used for personal data exchange and control, like syncing a phone to a laptop or connecting a headset.

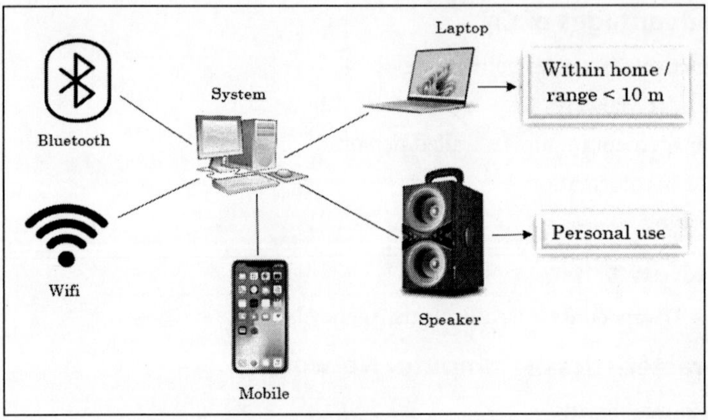

Fig. 1.2

2. LAN – Local Area Network

- Connects devices in a small, localized area like a home, office, or single building.
- Different devices (computers, printers, servers) share resources ina restricted area.
- It typically does not connect different LANs together directly, but can be a segment of a larger network.
- The range is typically less than 150 meters.

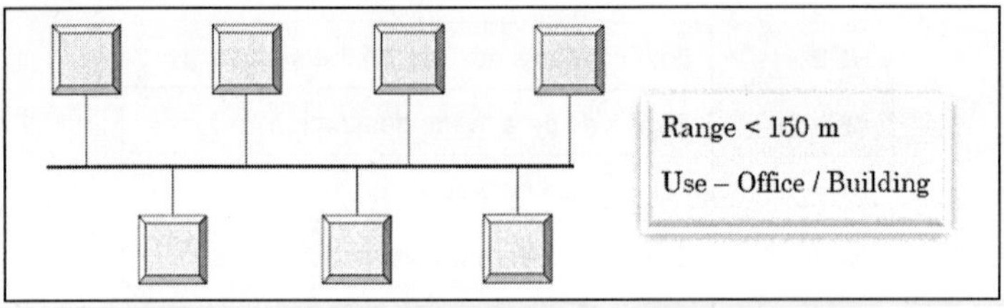

Fig. 1.3

3. MAN – Metropolitan Area Network

Collection of LANs

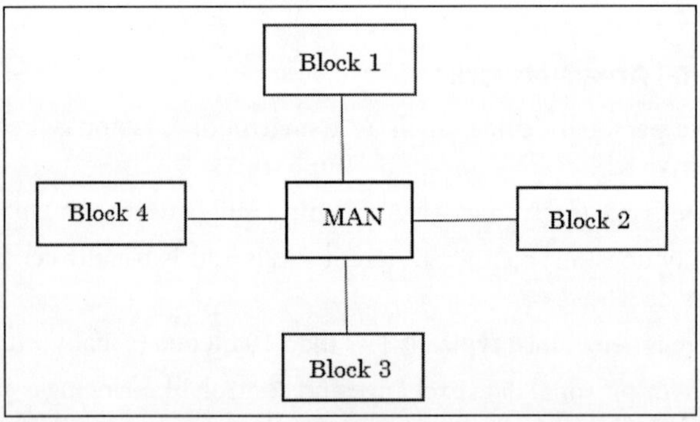

Fig. 1.4

- Connects different blocks in an enterprise.
- Different institutes in a city.
- It connects various LANs together.
- The range is < 50 km.
- Can be used within a city

WAN – Wide Area Network

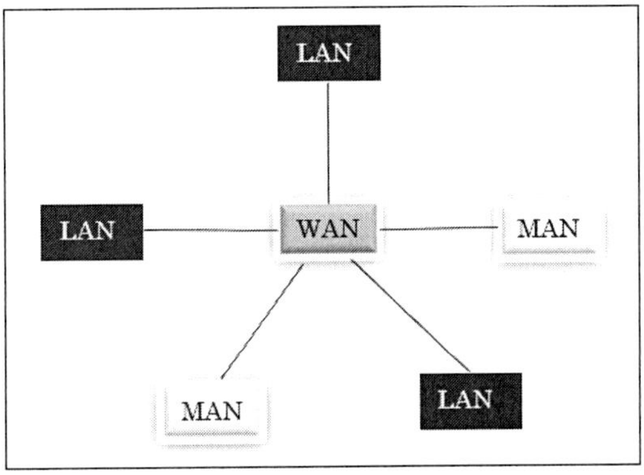

Fig. 1.5

- Connects various LAN / MAN.
- Connects various countries/networks in the world together.
- No limitation of range.

1.2 NETWORK TOPOLOGY

The physical and logical arrangement of nodes and connections in a network is called network topology.

Types

- Bus
- Ring
- Star
- Mesh
- Hybrid
- Tree
- Point to Point

1.2.1 Bus

- Every node is connected to a single cable.
- Bidirectional

Advantages

- Easy to add/remove the nodes.

- Less expensive
- Easy to maintain
- Failure of one device does not affect the other.

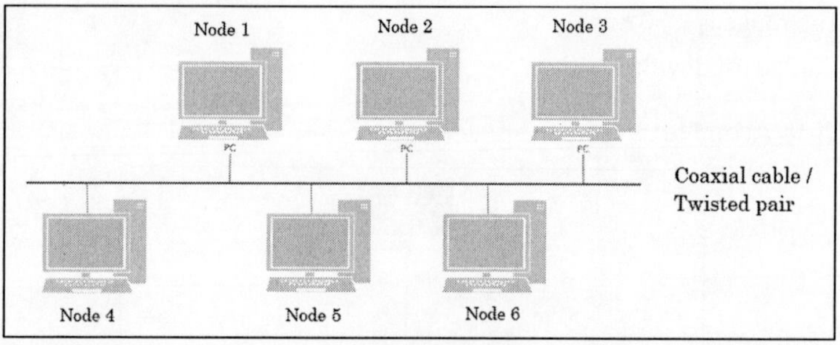

Fig. 1.6

Disadvantages

- Failure of cable leads to failure of the network.
- Every message is broadcasted so no private message is possible.
- Time-consuming to send a message.
- Limitation of cable length.

1.2.2. Ring

- Forms ring by connecting each node with an adjacent node.
- Data passes from each node to the adjacent node in a circular order.
- It is unidirectional.
- Repeaters are used to prevent data loss.

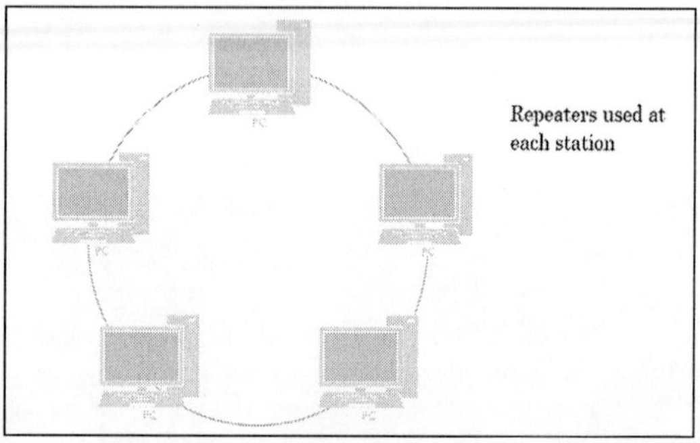

Fig. 1.7

- Data is passed using a token passing way from one node to the other.
- A token is the frame that circulates around the network.

Advantages

- The speed of transmission is high.
- The possibility of collision is less.

- Cheap to install and expand.
- Less costly compared to the Star Topology.

Disadvantages

- Failure of a single node causes entire nodes to fail.
- Difficult to troubleshoot.
- It is less secure.

1.2.3 Star

- All hosts are connected to a central device known as a hub device through cable
- Coaxial cables or RJ-45 cables are used to connect.

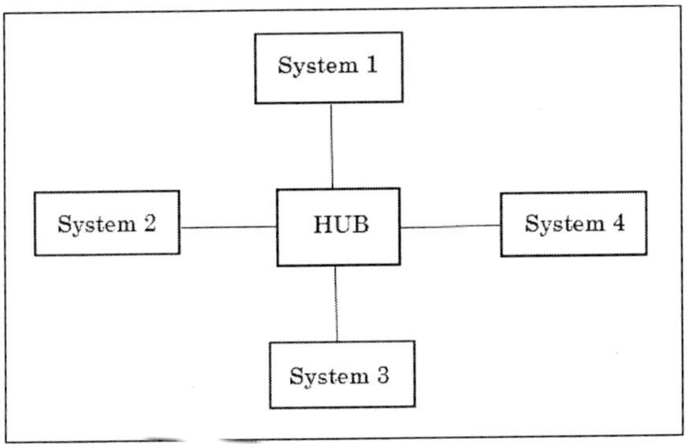

Fig. 1.8

Advantages

- Efficient troubleshooting
- Network control
- Limited failure
- Tools are cost-effective
- Easily expandable
- Data speed is high

Disadvantages

- If the hub fails whole system crashes.
- Installation cost is high.
- Performance is based on a single concentrator.

1.2.4 Mesh

- The arrangement of a network in which multiple paths exist from one computer to the other.
- The network is an example.
- No. of cables required = (n*(n–1)) / 2, where n = no. of nodes

Types of Mesh

- **Full mesh topology:** All computers are connected to each other.
- **Partially mesh topology:** Not all nodes, but few are connected to each other.

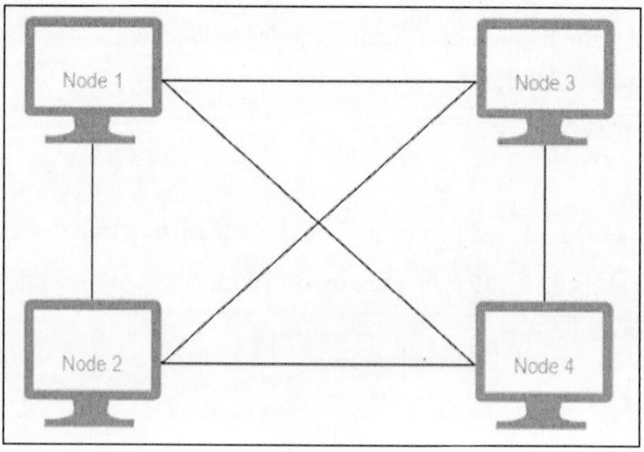

Fig. 1.9

Advantages

- Fast communication
- Robust
- Any fault is diagnosed easily.
- Provides security & privacy.

Disadvantages

- Installation & configuration is difficult.
- The cost is high.
- High maintenance is required.

1.2.5 Hybrid

- It is the combination of various types of topologies.

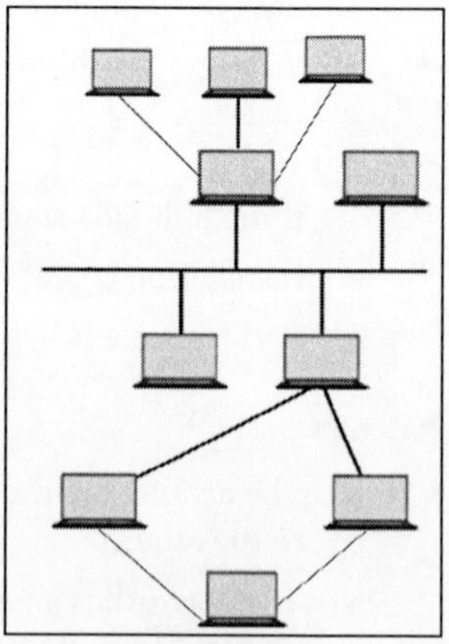

Fig. 1.10

Advantages

- Flexible
- Easy to add new devices
- Reliable

Disadvantages

- Challenging to design architecture.
- Hub is expensive.
- Infrastructure cost is high.

1.2.6 Tree

- It is a variation of star topology.
- Has a hierarchical flow of data.
- Protocols like DHCP & SAC (Standard Automatic Configuration) are used.

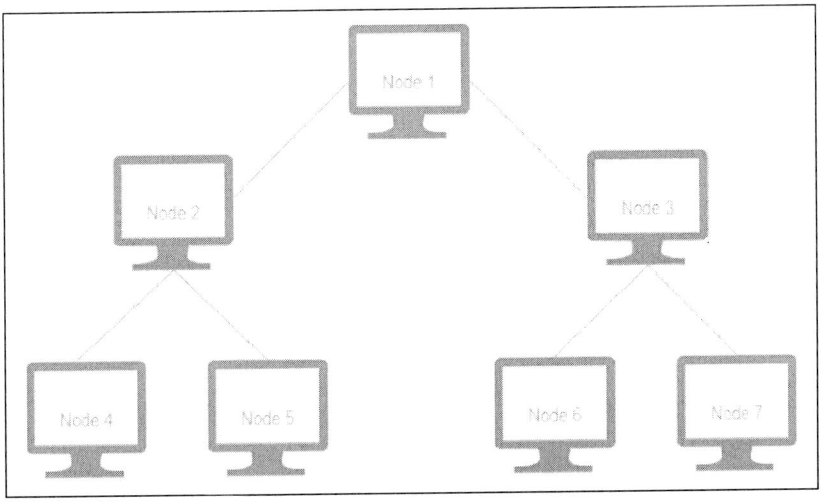

Fig. 1.11

- Various secondary hubs are connected to the central hub which contains the repeater.
- Data flows from a central hub to a secondary and then to the devices.

Advantages

- Allows many devices to the central hub.
- Allows the network to get isolated.
- Can add new devices to the existing network.
- Error detection and correction are easy.
- The breakdown of one station does not affect the entire network.

Disadvantages

- Difficulty in troubleshooting.
- Higher cost.
- Reconfiguration is difficult.

1.3 OSI LAYERS

- OSI - Open System Interconnection
- The model was created by ISO in 1984.
- It is a reference framework that explains the process of transmitting data between computers.

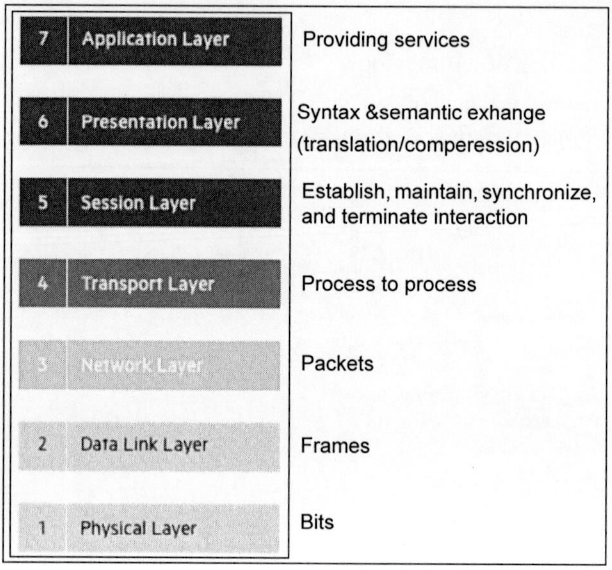

Fig 1.13

Physical Layer

- Transmits individual bits from one node to another node.
- Line configuration & data transmission.

Datalink Layer

- Error-free transfer of data frames.
- Reliable & efficient communication.
- Logical link control layer & Media Access Control Layer

HEADER	Packet (Data)	TRAILER

Functions

- Framing, physical addressing, flow control, error control, and access control.

Network Layer

- **Functions:** Inter-networking, logical connection between different devices.
- **Addressing:** Adds source and destination address to the header of the frame
- **Routing:** Determines optional path.
- **Packetizing:** Using Internet Protocol (IP), packets received from the upper layer are converted to packets.

Transport Layer

- Messages are transmitted in the order in which they are sent and no duplication of data.

- Converts data into units called segments.
- Transmission Control Protocol or User Datagram Protocol is used.
- Functions are service point addressing, segmentation & reassembly, connection control, flow control, and error control.

Session Layer

- **Functions:** Dialog control – half duplex or full duplex.
- Synchronization

Presentation Layer

- **Functions:** Translation, encryption, and compression.

Application Layer

- Provides network services to end users.
- File transfer, access, and management & mail services.

1.4 DESIGN PRINCIPLES

- To deliver services as requested by the user.
- Acceptable throughput & response time.
- Budget-friendly & maximizing cost efficiency.
- Reliability
- Expandable without major redesign.
- Maintenance & support
- Well documented
- Security

Steps

1. Verify the goal and technical requirements.
2. Determine the features and functions required.
3. Perform network readiness assessment.
4. Creating solutions & preparing test plans.
5. Create a project plan.

Factors Considered

1. Balancing distribution
2. Level of transparency
3. Security
4. Connectivity technology

1.5 NETWORK DESIGN APPROACHES

Top–Down Approach

- The requirements are considered first with applications & solutions next.

- Identifying name, service level agreement, and budget.
- Starts considering from application layer.

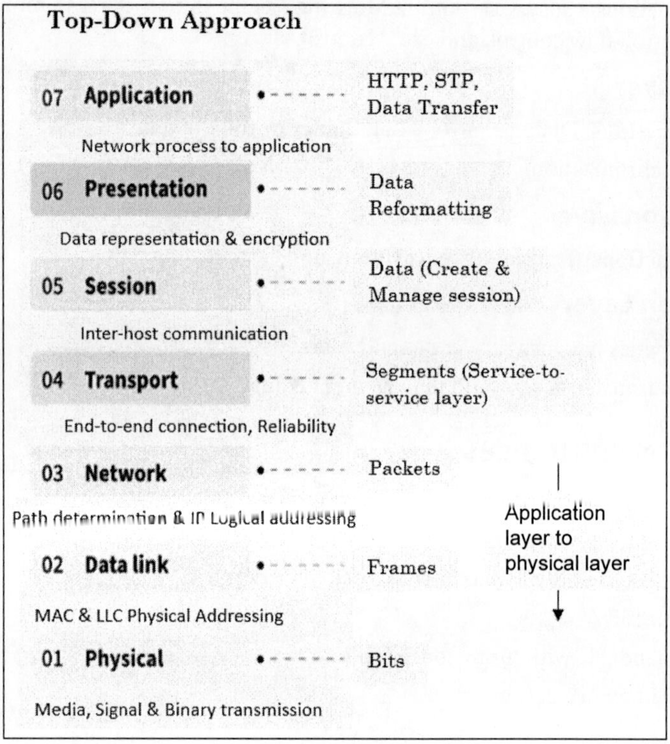

Fig. 1.13

Advantages

- Focuses on goals and requirements.

Disadvantages

- Requires thorough initial needs.
- Analysis in order to determine specific requirements and ensure all applications & services are considered.

Bottom-up Approach

Starts from the lower layer of the OSI model, which considers establishing a functional network first by deciding bandwidth, hardware, and security, then moves to applications.

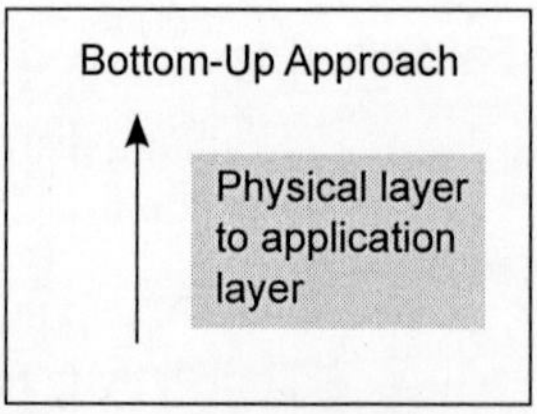

Fig. 1.14

Hierarchical Network Design

- It is the process of placing network devices that follow a hierarchical model.
- A network is designed such that a complex network of devices is broken into small and manageable areas.

- The network is divided into distinct layers. (Layers are called Tiers).
- They are divided into manageable blocks which limit local traffic.
- It can be used for both LAN and WAN.

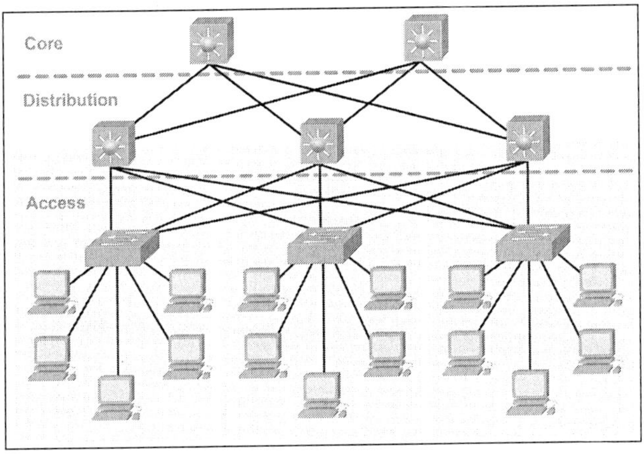

Fig. 1.15

1. Access Layer

- It consists of end users.
- It is referred to as network edge.
- This layer provides high bandwidth.
- Protects the network from malicious attacks.

2. Distribution Layer

- Policy-based connectivity.
- The boundary between the Access layer and the Core layer.
- It is responsible for collecting data from switches of the Access layer and distributing it to the rest of the network.
- Provides policy-based security using an Access Control List (ACL) and filtering.
- Provides redundancy & load balancing.

3. Core Layer

- It is the backbone of the network, i.e. protects the network by providing fast transport between switches in the distribution layer.
- Responsible for fast communication, reliability, and tolerance
- Connects multiple end networks together.

Advantages

- Large and complex networks are divided into smaller sub-networks.
- The local traffic remains local which increases network efficiency.
- It makes the network scalable.

Disadvantages

- Difficulty in evaluating the network.
- Scalability is not possible for larger networks.

Modular Network Design (CISCO N/W Architecture)

To overcome the difficulty of manageability & scalability, the network is split into smaller units with respect to physical, logical, and functional boundaries.

Guidelines

- Easy to deploy.
- Easy to manage.
- Flexible & scalable.
- Resilient & secure.

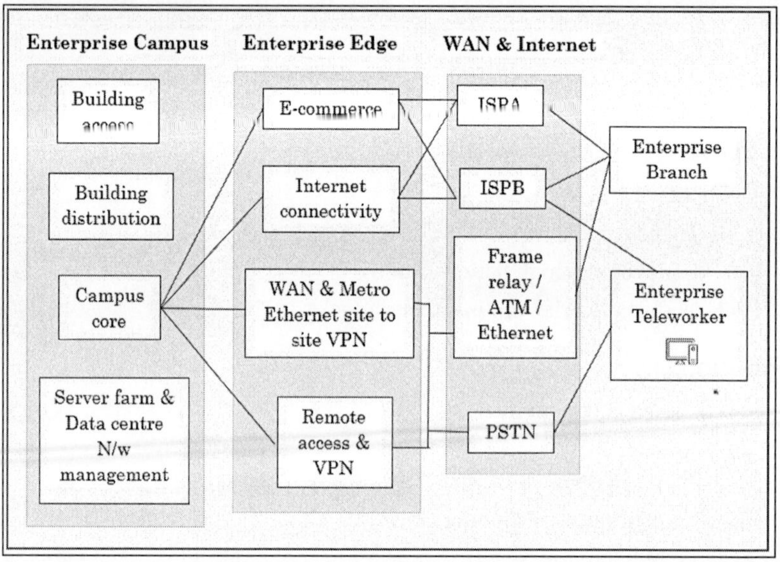

Fig. 1.16

Network Design Methodologies

1. Identifying Network Requirements

- Based on customer requirements, and the goal of the project, the network is designed.
- Business goals and technical requirements are focused.

2. Characterizing Existing Network

- Information about the current network and services is analyzed.
- The designer determines if existing equipment, infrastructure, and protocols can be reused and identifies new equipment and protocols.

3. Designing Network Topology

- The integration of existing infrastructure is maintained.
- Deployment of the network which is designed is also done.
- Designing is done with respect to the value of design, security measures, resilience, scalability, visibility, and sustainability.

Enterprise Campus	Enterprise Edge
Contains all functions required for independent operation within one campus location. E.g. Campus infrastructure, management module, server module, edge distribution module.	Contains all functions required for communication between enterprise campuses & remote locations.

Enterprise Campus

- *Building distribution module* provides access between workgroups and the core. Routing and filtering are done.
- *Management module* controls monitoring, logging, and security.
- The *network monitoring server* monitors devices on the network.
- *Management security* features that are implemented are:
  - *Authentication, Authorization, and Accounting (AAA)* server to provide security checks of users.
  - *Intrusion Detection System, Intrusion Prevention System* is used for network security.
  - System *logging* is used to log events straps using the Syslog server.
  - *Network management traffic* is used to traverse through in-band and out-of-band connections.

Server Module

- It contains a campus server.
- Has access to the server by implementing redundancy.
- High performance, filtering, and routing is achieved.

Edge Distribution Module

- The interface between enterprise campus and enterprise edge functional areas.

Enterprise Edge Functional Area

- The interface between Enterprise Campus and Enterprise Edge functional areas.
- Layer 3 switching provides high-performance routing.
- The *E-Commerce module* includes devices and services necessary for an organization which includes web servers, application servers, and security devices such as firewalls & IDS appliances.
- The *Internet module* provides internet access for users and passes VPN traffic from remote users to the VPN remote access module. E.g. servers are FTP, e-mail, DNS, firewalls.

- The <u>*WAN module*</u> provides connectivity between remote sites and the main site over WAN technology. E.g. Frame relay, Asynchronous Transfer Mode, (ATM), cable line, and leased line are some WAN interfaces.
- <u>*VPN / Remote Access module*</u> terminates VPN traffic and dial-in connections from external users. E.g. Dial-in access, VPN concentrators to terminate users in remote connections, firewalls, and IDS appliances.

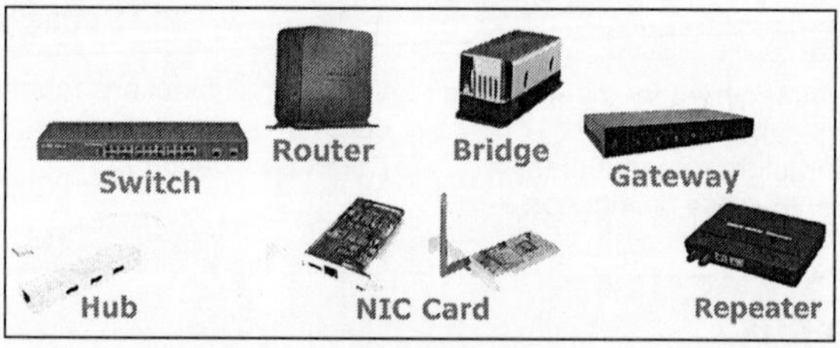

Fig. 1.17

Service Provider Edge Functional Area

- The <u>*Internet Service Provider (ISP) module*</u> represents connections to the Internet redundant connections to multiple ISPs can be made to ensure service availability.
- The <u>*Public Switched Telephone Network (PSTN) module*</u> represents all dial-up connectivity, including analog phones, cellular phones, and ISDN.
- <u>*Frame Relay / ATM module*</u> represents all permanent connections to remote locations including Frame Relay and ATM.

1.6 NETWORK DEVICES

(Networking Hardware, Network Equipment)

Hub

Hub is a physical layer device which has multiple ports that are used to connect multiple computers or segments of LAN together.

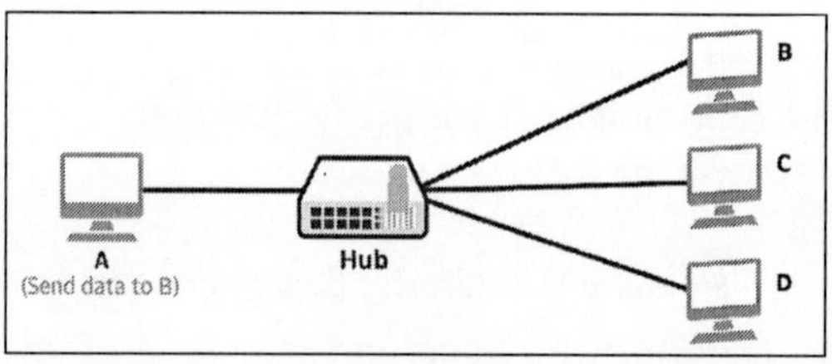

Fig. 1.18

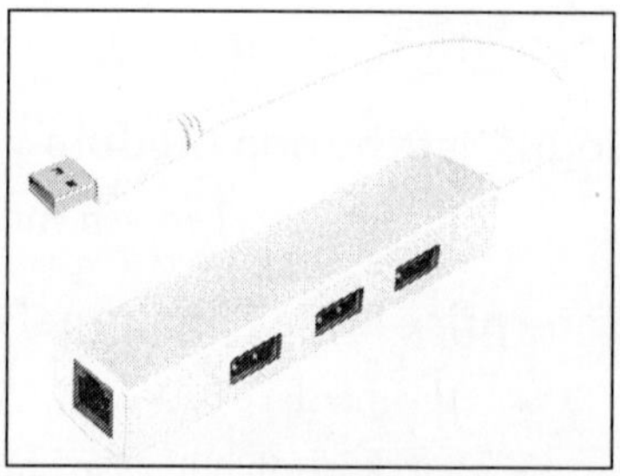

Fig. 1.19

Switch

Hub just does the work of data forwarding, a switch does **"Filter and Forwarding"** which is a more intelligent way of dealing with the data packets.

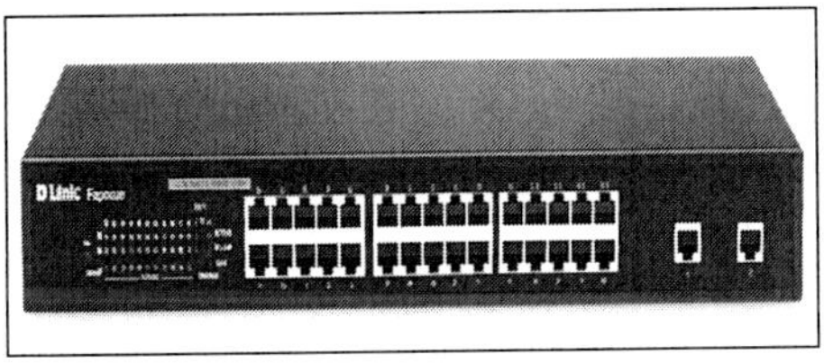

Fig. 1.20

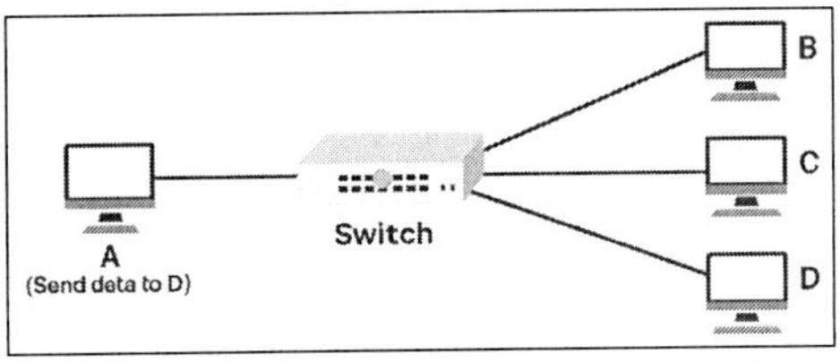

Fig. 1.21

Router

The router is mainly a Network Layer device. It can work like a switch that routes data packets based on their IP addresses.

Fig. 1.22

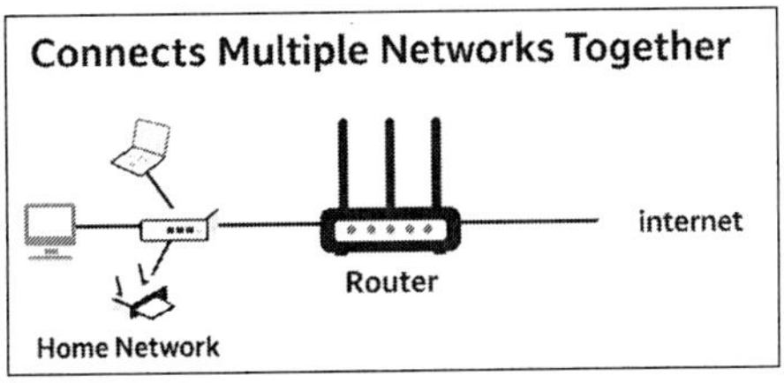

Fig. 1.23

Difference between Hub, Switch and Routers

Hub	Switch	Router
• Works in the Physical Layer	• Data / Network Layer	• Network Layer
• Broadcast messages.	• Multicast messages.	• Routes messages.
• Sends data as Bits.	• Sends data as Frames.	• Sends data as Packets.
• Connect devices within the same network.	• Connect devices to the network.	• Connect two different networks.
• Does not store MAC addresses.	• Store MAC addresses.	• Store MAC addresses.

Bridge

A bridge connects two or more LANs. It operates at the data link layer. Bridges handle networks that follow the same protocol.

Functions

- Filtering, Forwarding, Blocking

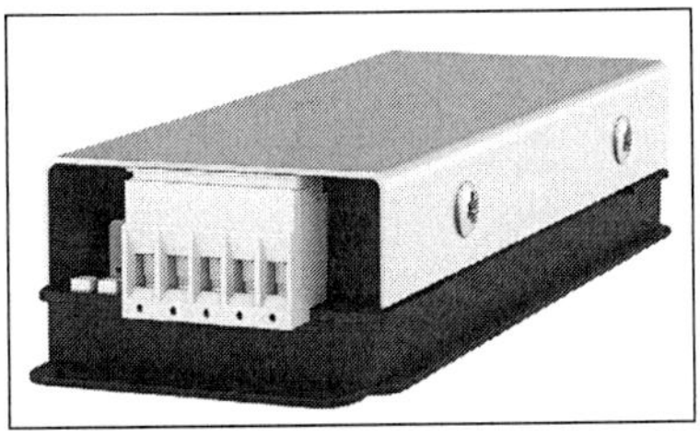

Fig. 1.24

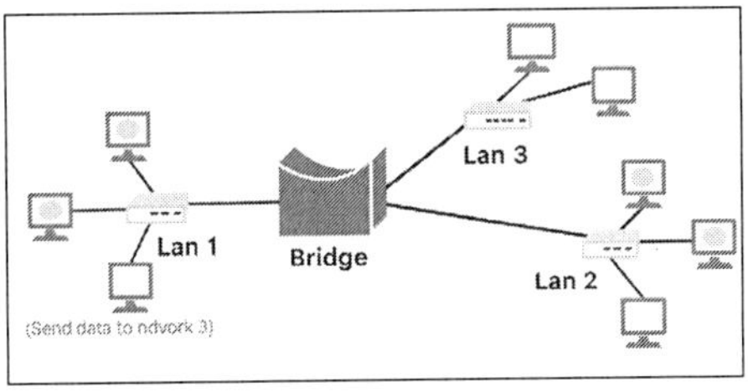

Fig. 1.25

Gateway

A gateway is a network device used to connect two or more dissimilar networks.

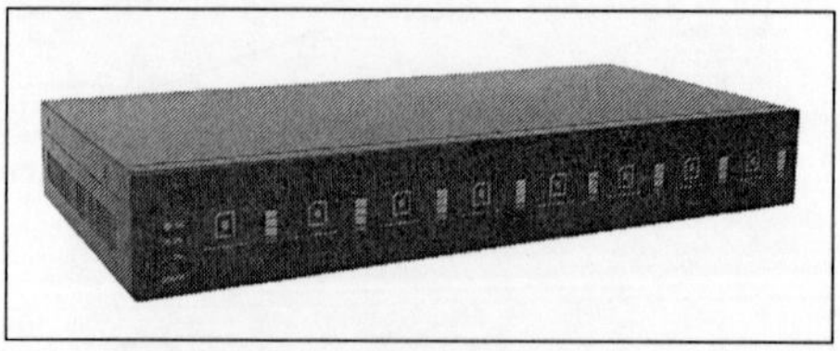

Fig. 1.26

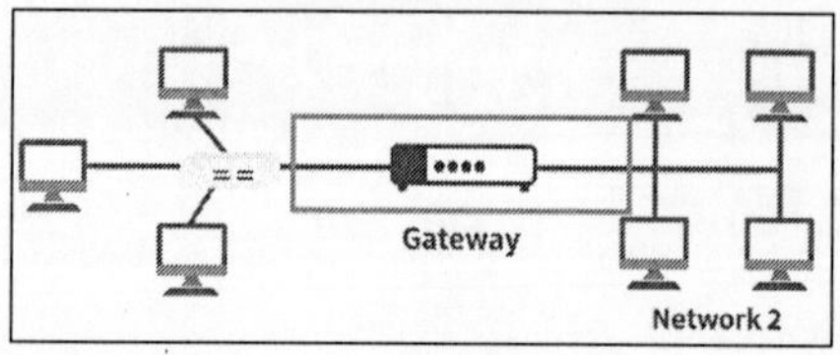

Fig. 1.27

Repeater

Repeaters are used to extend transmissions so that the signal can cover longer distances or be received on the other side of an obstruction.

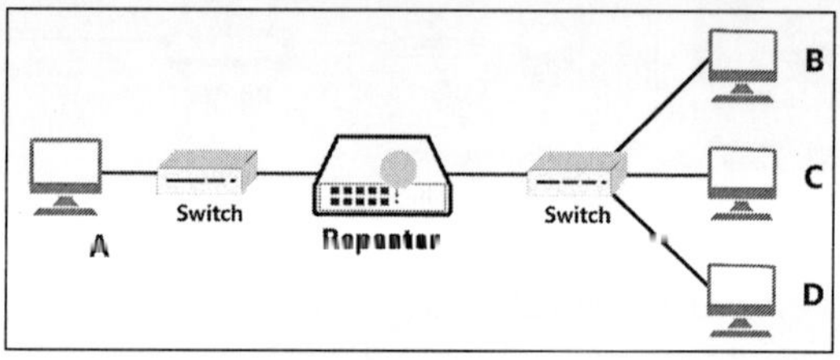

Fig. 1.28

Network Interface Card (NIC)

It is a physical and data link layer device used by computers to connect and communicate with other devices on the LAN.

E.g. Ethernet card, Network card, LAN card, Network Adapter Card (NAC) or Network Interface Unit (NIU), or Terminal Access Point (TAP).

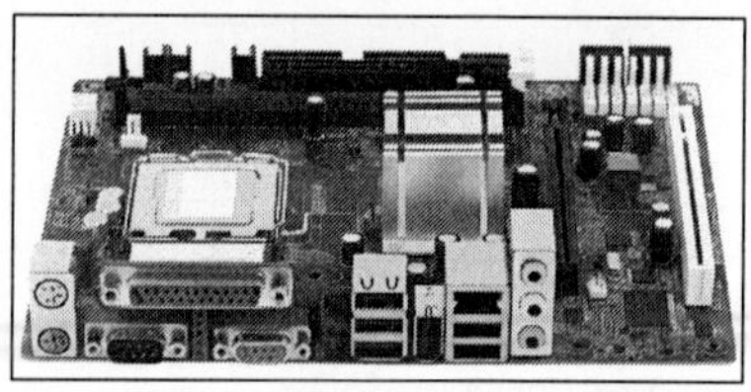

Fig. 1.29

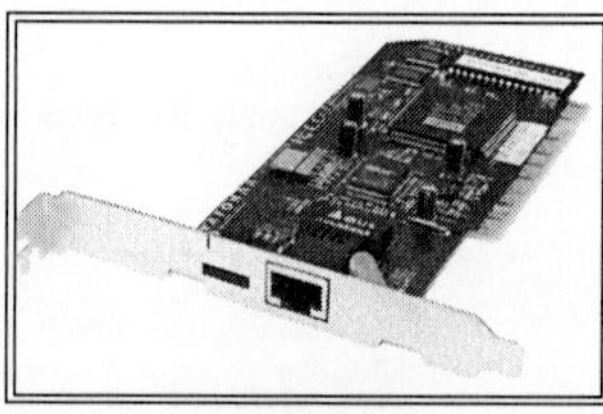

Fig. 1.30

Fig. 1.31

Wi-Fi (Wireless Fidelity) Card

Wi-Fi card is used to connect any device to a local network wirelessly.

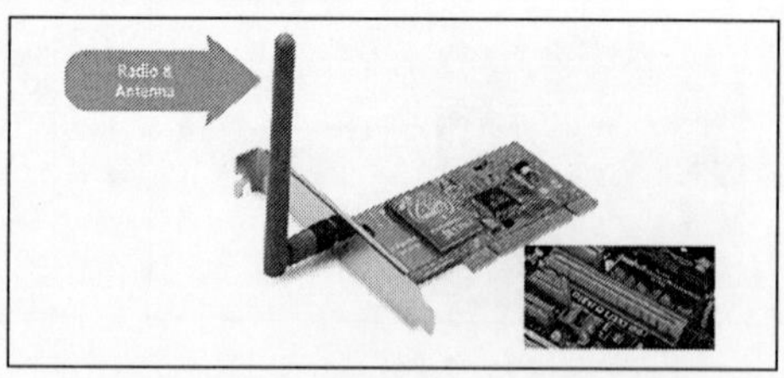

Fig. 1.32

Access Point (WAP)

The physical area of the network that provides internet access through Wi-Fi is called a Wi-Fi hotspot or Wi-Fi Access Point.

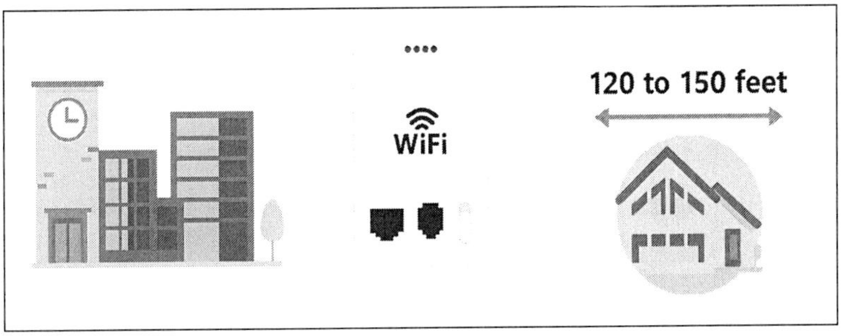

Fig. 1.33

SUMMARY

- **Efficiency, Scalability, and Security:** A structured network design ensures optimal performance and future growth.
- **Determining Requirements:** Aligns the network with business needs and objectives.
- **Analyzing the Existing Network:** Identifies gaps, inefficiencies, and areas for improvement.
- **Preparing a Preliminary Design:** Lays the foundation for a well-structured network.
- **Final Design Development and Deployment:** Ensures seamless integration and functionality.
- **Monitoring and Redesigning:** Optimizes performance and adapts to changing needs.
- **Maintenance:** Ensures long-term reliability and efficiency.
- **Design Documentation:** Facilitates troubleshooting and future upgrades.
- **Modular and Hierarchical Network Designs:** Enhance scalability, manageability, and resilience.
- **Supporting Business Growth:** Creates a structured and future-proof network infrastructure.

EXERCISES

A. Subjective Questions

Category-I *(Revised Bloom's Levels-1, 2 & 3 – Remembering, Understanding, Applying)*

1. Define network design principles and explain their importance.
2. What are the key factors to consider when determining network requirements?
3. Describe the process of analyzing an existing network.
4. Explain the role of a preliminary network design in the overall design process.
5. How does hierarchical network design improve network efficiency and management?

6. What is modular network design? How does it help in scalability and flexibility?
7. Describe the importance of design documentation in network planning.
8. What are the key steps involved in deploying a network successfully?
9. Explain the role of network monitoring and redesigning in maintaining network performance.
10. Discuss different network maintenance strategies and their significance.

Category-II ***(Revised Bloom's Levels-4, 5 & 6 – Analyzing, Evaluating, Creating)***

1. Analyze the challenges faced while determining network requirements and propose solutions.
2. Compare and contrast modular and hierarchical network designs. Which is more effective and why?
3. Evaluate the impact of improper network documentation on troubleshooting and future upgrades.
4. Develop a case study-based scenario where network redesign is necessary and suggest a redesign plan.
5. Justify the importance of monitoring and proactive redesigning in preventing network failures.
6. How would you optimize network deployment to ensure minimal downtime and maximum efficiency?
7. Critically analyze the difference between preliminary and final network design stages with examples.
8. Propose a structured maintenance plan for a large-scale enterprise network.
9. Examine a real-world scenario where a poorly designed network led to inefficiencies. Suggest improvements based on design principles.
10. Create a checklist for deploying a new network infrastructure while ensuring security, scalability, and manageability.

B. Objective Questions

Category-I ***(Revised Bloom's Levels-1, 2 & 3 – Remembering, Understanding, Applying)***

1. Which of the following is NOT a key principle of network design?
   (a) Scalability (b) Security
   (c) Random Deployment (d) Manageability
2. What is the first step in the network design process?
   (a) Analyzing the existing network (b) Determining requirements
   (c) Deploying the network (d) Creating documentation
3. Which network design model divides a network into core, distribution, and access layers?
   (a) Modular Design (b) Hierarchical Design
   (c) Flat Network Design (d) Peer-to-Peer Design

4. What is the purpose of network monitoring?
   (a) To identify performance issues
   (b) To increase security risks
   (c) To replace network hardware frequently
   (d) To avoid using modular designs
5. Why is modular network design beneficial?
   (a) It increases redundancy and complexity
   (b) It allows for easier scaling and troubleshooting
   (c) It prevents network expansion
   (d) It eliminates the need for security measures
6. The preliminary network design phase involves:
   (a) Implementing the network
   (b) Identifying basic architecture and components
   (c) Replacing old hardware
   (d) Skipping documentation
7. What is the primary goal of network maintenance?
   (a) Ignoring minor issues
   (b) Ensuring long-term reliability and performance
   (c) Increasing network downtime
   (d) Avoiding network redesign
8. Which document records all network configurations and design decisions?
   (a) Final Report (b) Design Documentation
   (c) User Manual (d) Maintenance Log
9. A well-structured network should be:
   (a) Rigid and difficult to expand (b) Easily scalable and manageable
   (c) Expensive with unnecessary hardware (d) Disorganized and undocumented
10. What is a key feature of a hierarchical network design?
   (a) All devices directly connect to each other
   (b) The network is divided into logical layers
   (c) There is no distinction between different network levels
   (d) The network does not require redundancy

Ans.: 1. (c), 2. (b), 3. (b), 4. (a), 5. (b), 6. (b), 7. (b), 8. (b), 9. (b), 10. (b)

Category-II *(Revised Bloom's Levels-4, 5 & 6 – Analyzing, Evaluating, Creating)*

1. A company is facing network congestion issues. Which strategy would best address this?
   (a) Ignoring the issue
   (b) Implementing hierarchical design principles
   (c) Increasing network complexity
   (d) Removing network monitoring tools

2. When redesigning an outdated network, what is the most crucial factor to consider?
   (a) Cost and downtime
   (b) Randomly selecting new hardware
   (c) Ignoring security enhancements
   (d) Avoiding user feedback
3. A company has a rapidly growing workforce. How should the network design be modified?
   (a) Adopt a flat network structure
   (b) Implement modular network design for scalability
   (c) Limit network expansion
   (d) Reduce security measures to improve speed
4. A network administrator notices frequent bottlenecks in the core layer. What should be done?
   (a) Ignore the issue
   (b) Analyze traffic patterns and optimize design
   (c) Increase hardware without assessment
   (d) Remove network monitoring tools
5. In which scenario would a modular design be more beneficial than a flat network?
   (a) A small office with five computers
   (b) A growing enterprise with multiple branches
   (c) A single-user home network
   (d) A peer-to-peer gaming setup
6. What is the best approach for a smooth network deployment process?
   (a) Implementing without testing
   (b) Following a phased deployment with testing
   (c) Deploying all components simultaneously
   (d) Ignoring documentation and monitoring
7. How can proactive network monitoring help prevent failures?
   (a) By identifying and resolving potential issues before they escalate
   (b) By making troubleshooting more difficult
   (c) By reducing security measures to improve performance
   (d) By eliminating the need for network maintenance
8. A company wants to upgrade its network without disrupting operations. What should they do?
   (a) Perform a staged deployment with backup plans
   (b) Replace all hardware at once
   (c) Shut down the network during work hours
   (d) Avoid informing employees about the changes
9. How would you evaluate whether a network design is effective?
   (a) By assessing scalability, security, and performance metrics
   (b) By ensuring only the cheapest equipment is used

(c) By limiting documentation to save time

(d) By designing without considering future needs

10. If a network experiences frequent failures, what is the best approach to redesign?

(a) Investigate root causes and implement improvements

(b) Replace all equipment without analysis

(c) Ignore the issue and hope for better performance

(d) Remove redundancy to simplify the design

Ans.: 1. (b), 2. (a), 3. (b), 4. (b), 5. (b), 6. (b), 7. (a), 8. (a), 9. (a), 10. (a)

TEACHER'S KNOW MORE

- **Design Principles:** Focus on scalability, security, reliability, and efficiency in network architecture.
- **Determining Requirements:** Gather business and technical needs to ensure network alignment with organizational goals.
- **Analyzing the Existing Network:** Assess current infrastructure, identify bottlenecks, and evaluate performance metrics.
- **Preparing the Preliminary Design:** Outline a high-level architecture, including topology, device selection, and redundancy planning.
- **Completing the Final Design Development:** Finalize hardware, software, security policies, and integration strategies.
- **Deploying the Network:** Implement the network in a structured, phased approach to minimize disruptions.
- **Monitoring and Redesigning:** Continuously track network performance, identify issues, and make improvements.
- **Maintaining the Network:** Regular updates, troubleshooting, and security patches to ensure smooth operation.
- **Design Documentation:** Maintain detailed records of configurations, policies, and changes for future reference.
- **Modular Network Design:** Enhances flexibility, scalability, and troubleshooting efficiency by structuring networks into modules.
- **Hierarchical Network Design:** Divides networks into core, distribution, and access layers for better management and performance.

This page is intentionally left blank!

2

UNIT

Underlying LAN Concepts

RATIONALE

This unit focuses on LAN connectivity for small businesses, covering essential networking technologies such as Token Ring, Ethernet, and ATM LAN emulation. It explores strategies for network integration, InterLAN switching, and LAN-to-mainframe connectivity, ensuring seamless communication between systems. Also provides insights into building scalable and efficient networks, equipping learners with the knowledge to design, implement, and optimize local area networks (LANs) for enhanced performance, reliability, and business growth.

OUTCOMES

- **Understanding LAN Technologies and Integration**: Gain knowledge of various LAN connectivity methods such as Ethernet, Token Ring, ATM LAN emulation, and InterLAN Switching, and their role in small business networking.
- **Implementing and Managing Network Solutions**: Learn how to design, integrate, and maintain LAN connections, including LAN-to-mainframe communication and network building strategies for seamless business operations.

2.1 LAN

A Local Area Network is a group of computers and peripheral devices that are connected together within a distinct geographic area such as a building, campus, or enterprise. The devices are connected by a common communication line or wireless connection to a server.

LAN includes various network components such as cables, switches, routers, firewalls, load balancers, and wireless access points. It can be connected to a wide range of network devices like game consoles, servers, desktops, laptops, printers, and Internet of Things devices.

- Each device on the LAN is assigned a unique internet protocol address.
- An IP address is mapped to a physical address called the Media Access Control Address on each device.
- Ethernet switches use this to direct data across the network.
- Ethernet and Wi-Fi are primary ways to enable LAN connections.

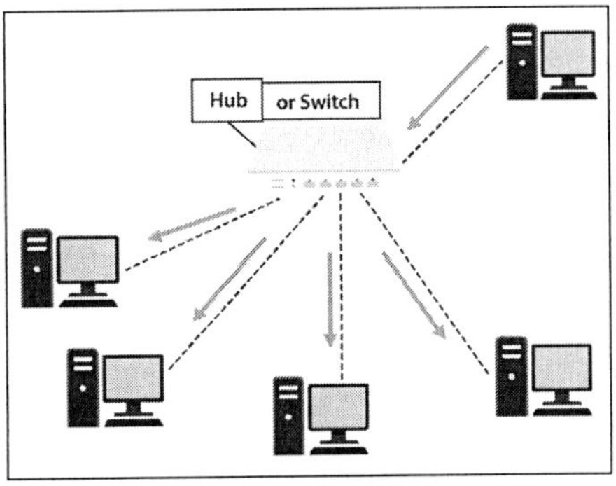

Fig. 2.1

2.1.1 Benefits of LAN

- Using a single internet connection, can share files with one another.
- Centralized access to resources.
- Efficient communication
- Shared internet connection
- Data protection
- Fast communication

2.2 TYPES OF LAN

- **Peer-to-peer:** 2 devices connected directly
- **Client-server:** multiple devices are connected to the server
- Ethernet
- **Token ring:** traditional access speed 100 Mbps
- Asynchronous Transfer Mode
- **Cloud Managed:** Centralized cloud platform to oversee access control, policy enforcement, security, and network use in a heterogeneous network environment.

2.2.1 Ethernet-widely used LAN

- Use coaxial, twisted pair copper, and fibre optic cables.
- Each device is physically connected to an ethernet switch or router.
- Twisted pair ethernet cable with RJ458 pin connectors.

Ethernet is a communication standard developed in the early 80's to network computers and other devices in a local environment (Local Area Network).

LAN connects multiple devices to create, store, and share information with other devices. Ethernet was standardized into standard IEEE 8023 in 1983 by the Institute of Electrical and Electronic Engineering.

- Ethernet IEEE 8023 defined the Physical layer and Datalink layer of wired Ethernet.
- The physical layer has cabling and devices.
- Media Access Control of Datalink layer.

2.3 TRANSMISSION MEDIA

The raw data which is transported is transmitted through the transmission media which is either guided or unguided.

- **Guided:** Data is transmitted through the cabling system that has a fixed path.

  E.g. Copper wire, and fibre optic wires.
- **Unguided:** Data travels through free space as an electromagnetic signal.

  E.g. Radio waves, lasers, etc.,

2.3.1 Twisted Pair Cable

Invented by Alexander Graham Bell in 1881. It has two conductors made of copper and has insulation. These conductors are twisted together.

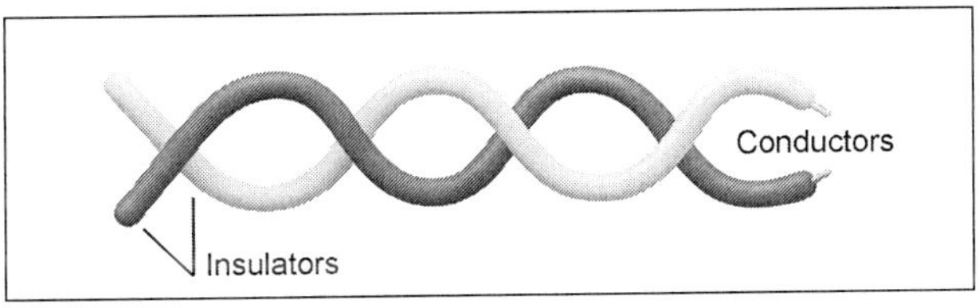

Fig. 2.2: Twisted Pair Cables

- One carries the signal and the other is used for ground reference. The receiver uses the difference of signals between these two conductors.
- The twist of the cable is to avoid noise.
- The quality depends on the number of twists per unit length of the cable.

2.3.1.1 Types of Twisted Pair

1. Unshielded Twisted Pair Cables (UTP)

- A pair of two insulated copper wires twisted together without any consultation.
- Insulation reduces external interference.

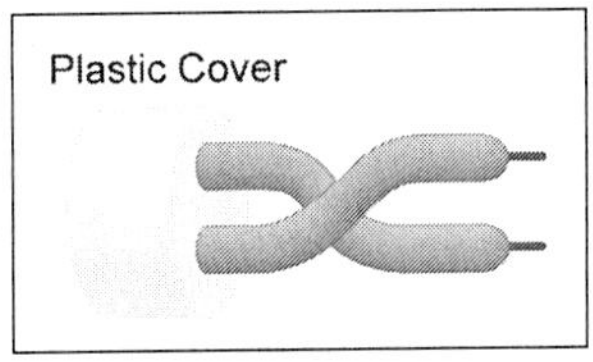

Fig. 2.3

Advantages

- Cost-effective and easy to install.
- Used for shorter distances.
- Used for both analog and digital transmissions.
- It does not affect the entire network if part of the network is damaged.

Disadvantages

- Need repeaters for longer distances.
- Error rate increases if distance > 100 m.
- Thin and breaks easily.
- Not used for broadband connection.

2. Shielded Twisted Pair Cables (STP)

- Each twisted pair is scheduled.
- The covering provides strength to the overall structure of the cable.
- Shielding ensures induced signal can be returned to the source by ground and circulates around the shield without affecting the main propagatory signal.

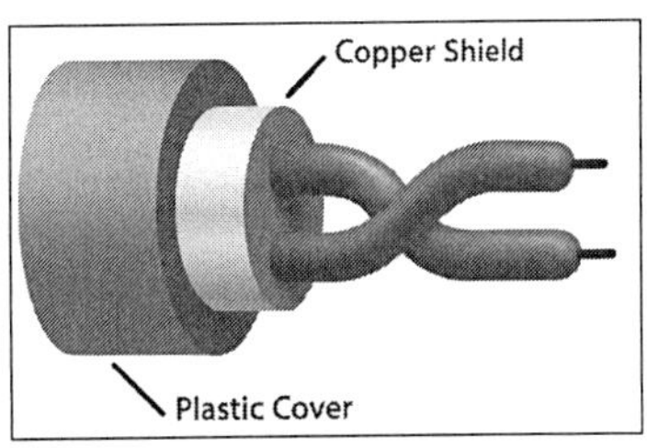

Fig. 2.4

Advantages

- Used for long-distance communication and installed underground.
- A protective shield prevents external electromagnetic noise penetration into the cable.
- It has a higher bandwidth.

Disadvantages

- Expensive
- Requires lot of maintenance
- Installed underground
- Length similar to UTP

2.3.1.2 Application of Twisted Pair Cable

- Twisted pair cable is used in telephone lines.
- LAN
- Both analog & digital transmission of signals
- RJ-45 common cable

2.3.2 Coaxial Cable

- Used by cable operators, telephone companies, and internet providers to transmit data, video & voice.
- Installation and implementation are easy.
- Provides moderately high bandwidth.
- Made of plastic & copper wire to transmit signal in electrical form rather than light form.
- Core copper conductor transmits signals & insulators provide insulation to copper conductors. (data transmission).
- An insulator is surrounded by a braided metal conductor which prevents interference of electrical signals and prevents cross talk. (barrier against EMI).
- The entire setup is covered by protective EMI - Electro Magnetic Interference.
- Plastic layer to ensure safety of cable (protects internal layer from damage).

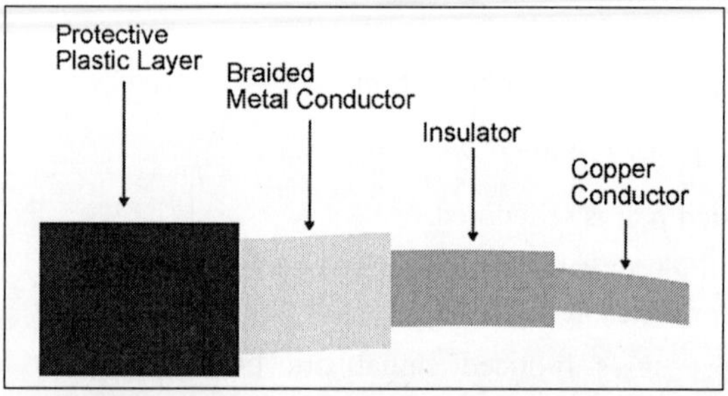

Fig. 2.5

Types

- **Broadband transmission** (transmits multiple signals simultaneously) **and**
- **Baseband transmission** (transmits single signal, high speed)
  - Hardline coaxial cable
  - Semi-rigid coaxial cable
  - Flexible coaxial cable

- Formable coaxial cable
- Twin axial coaxial cable
- Triaxial coaxial cable
- Rigid coaxial cable

Advantages

- Coaxial cable provides high bandwidth.
- Easy to install
- Reliable & durable
- Less affected by noise
- Supports multiple channels.

Disadvantages

- Expensive
- Must be grounded to prevent crosstalk.
- It has multiple layers.
- Chances of breaking

2.3.3 Fiber Optics

- It transmits data as light pulses along a glass or plastic fibre.
- Optical fibre is cylindrical fibre of glass which is hair thin.
- It is used for optical communication; it's waveguides are made of transparent dielectrics.
- Used for long-distance and high-performance data networking.

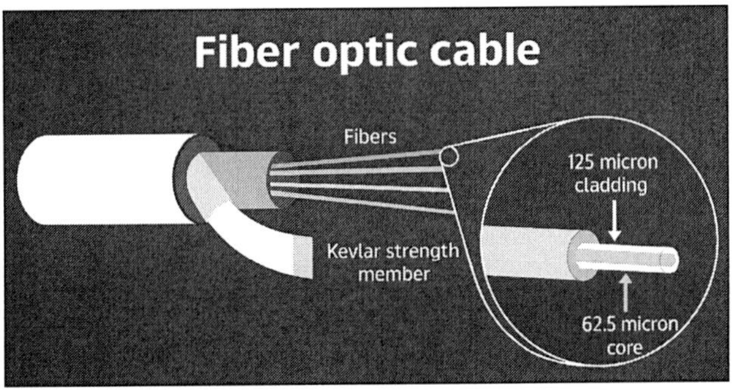

Fig. 2.6

- **Light-emitting diodes** (LEDs) or **Laser Diodes** (LDs) emit light waves at the source, which are read by detectors at the other end.
- It has a core central tube which is very thin and made of optically transparent dielectric medium and carries a light transmitter to the receiver.
- **Cladding** is outer optical material surrounding the core having a reflecting index lower than the core and cladding keeps light within the core.
- Buffer coating is a plastic coating that protects fibre made of silicon rubber

Types

- **Single-mode fibre**: Only one type of ray of light can propagate through fibre.
- **Multi-mode fibre**: many modes of light rays travel. Signal degradation occurs due to multimode dispersion.
- **Types:** Step index fibres and graded index fibre.

Advantages

- Supports high bandwidth
- Electromagnetic interference is protected
- Faster speed as cable carries data in form of light
- Longer distance
- Better reliability
- Thinner and sturdier

Disadvantages

- Costlier than copper wire
- Manual work to install new cable
- Optical fibre requires more protection
- More fragile

2.3.3 Difference Between Coaxial Cable and Optical Fiber

Coaxial Cable	Optical Fibre
• Coaxial Cable is used to transmit the signal/data which is in electrical form.	• Optical Fiber is used to transmit the signal/data which is in light form.
• The diameter of the Coaxial cable is larger as compared to the optical fibre.	• The diameter of Optical fibre is small.
• The cost of coaxial cable is less.	• The cost of optical fibre is high.
• Coaxial cable is heavier than optical fibre in weight.	• Optical cable is lighter in weight.

2.4 OSI MODEL

The **Open Systems Interconnection (OSI) model** is a conceptual framework used to standardize and understand how different networking protocols and technologies interact in a networked environment.

Developed by the International Organization for Standardization (ISO) in 1984, the OSI model divides the communication process into seven distinct layers, each with specific functions and responsibilities. This layered approach ensures interoperability between different systems and simplifies troubleshooting.

The Seven Layers of the OSI Model

Layer -7	**Application Layer**	Human computer Interaction
Layer -6	**Presentation Layer**	Ensures that the data is in usable format
Layer -5	**Session Layer**	Responsible for controlling ports and sessions
Layer -4	**Transport Layer**	Transmits data using UDP and TCP
Layer -3	**Network Layer**	Decides the path of data
Layer -2	**Data-Link Layer**	Defines Data format
Layer -1	**Physical Layer**	Transmits the data over a physical medium in terms of bits

1. Physical Layer

The **Physical Layer** is the foundational layer of the OSI model, responsible for directly transmitting raw data bits between devices over a physical medium. It handles the establishment, maintenance, and termination of physical connections, ensuring that data can move reliably from one node to another. This layer also defines the mechanical, electrical, and procedural standards for network interfaces.

It inclues the following rules:

- It facilitates the actual transmission of bits over a physical medium, such as cables, fiber optics, or wireless channels.
- It ensures that the physical connection between devices is established and maintained for reliable communication.
- It adheres to mechanical and electrical specifications, such as cable types, connectors, and voltage levels, to enable seamless data transfer.

Functions

1. Line Configuration

Determines how devices are physically connected, whether in a point-to-point or multipoint configuration.

2. Data Transmission

Specifies the mode of data transfer between devices, which can be simplex (one-way), half-duplex (two-way, but not simultaneously), or full-duplex (two-way simultaneously).

3. Topology

Defines the arrangement of devices in a network, such as bus, star, ring, or mesh topologies.

4. Signals

Determines the type of signals used for data transmission, such as electrical, optical, or radio waves, and ensures proper encoding and decoding of these signals.

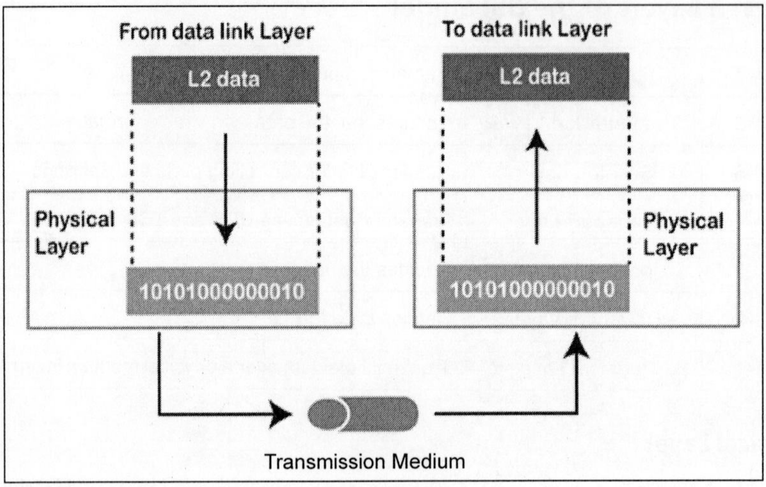

Fig. 2.7

2. Data Link Layer (Layer 2)

The Data Link Layer ensures the error-free transfer of data frames between devices on the same network. It defines the format of data and provides reliable communication by uniquely identifying devices on a local network. This layer is divided into two sub-layers:

1. **Logical Link Control (LLC):**
   - Transfers packets to the Network Layer of the receiving device.
   - Identifies the network layer protocol from the header.
   - Manages flow control to regulate data transmission.
2. **Media Access Control (MAC):**
   - Acts as a bridge between the LLC and the Physical Layer.
   - Controls how devices access the network and transmit data.

Functions

- **Framing:** Converts raw bit streams from the Physical Layer into structured frames. Adds headers (containing source and destination addresses) and trailers to each frame.
- **Physical Addressing:** Includes hardware addresses (MAC addresses) in the frame header to ensure delivery to the correct device.
- **Flow Control:** Maintains a consistent data rate between sender and receiver to prevent data overflow or corruption.
- **Error Control:** Uses techniques like CRC (Cyclic Redundancy Check) to detect and retransmit corrupted frames.
- **Access Control:** Determines which device has control over the network when multiple devices are connected.

HEADER	PACKET	TAILER

3. Network Layer (Layer 3)

The Network Layer manages device addressing, routing, and forwarding of data packets across different networks. It determines the optimal path for data transmission based on network conditions and service priorities.

Functions

- **Internetworking:** Establishes logical connections between devices across multiple networks.
- **Addressing:** Adds source and destination IP addresses to packet headers for identification.
- **Routing:** Selects the best path for data transmission using routing protocols.
- **Packetizing:** Converts data from the Transport Layer into packets for transmission.

4. Transport Layer (Layer 4)

The Transport Layer ensures reliable, end-to-end communication by managing data segmentation, error control, and flow control. It provides a point-to-point connection between the source and destination. It works based on two protocols namely:

- **TCP (Transmission Control Protocol):** Reliable, connection-oriented communication.
- **UDP (User Datagram Protocol):** Faster, connectionless communication with no error recovery.

Functions

- **Segmentation and Reassembly:** Divides data into smaller units (segments) and reassembles them at the destination.
- **Connection Control:** Offers both connection-oriented (TCP) and connectionless (UDP) services.
- **Flow Control:** Regulates data flow to prevent overwhelming the receiver.
- **Error Control:** Ensures data integrity by detecting and retransmitting lost or corrupted segments.

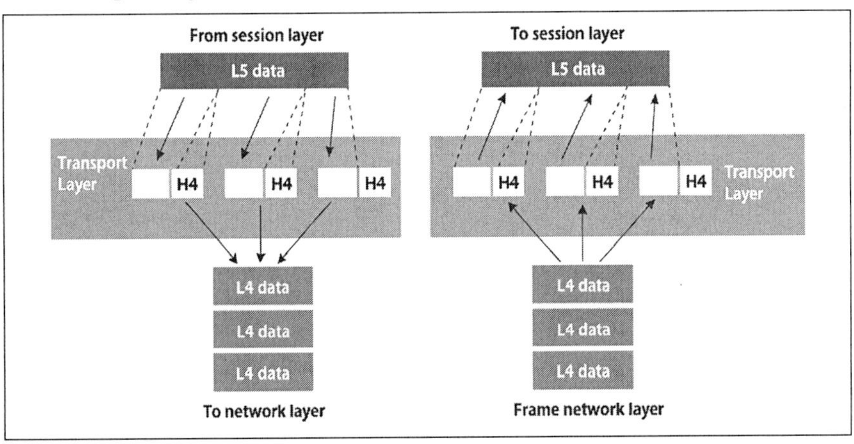

Fig. 2.8

Advantages of the Transport Layer

1. **Reliable Data Transmission:** Ensures data is delivered accurately and in the correct sequence using protocols like TCP (Transmission Control Protocol).
2. **Error Detection and Correction:** Identifies and corrects errors during data transmission, improving communication reliability.
3. **Flow Control:** Manages data flow between sender and receiver to prevent congestion and data loss.
4. **Segmentation and Reassembly:** Breaks large data packets into smaller segments and reassembles them at the destination.
5. **Multiplexing and Demultiplexing:** Allows multiple applications to use network services simultaneously by assigning unique ports.
6. **End-to-End Communication:** Establishes a direct connection between sender and receiver, ensuring efficient data delivery.
7. **Congestion Control:** Regulates network traffic to avoid overload and optimize performance.

Disadvantages of the Transport Layer

1. **Increased Overhead:** Implementing features like error control, flow control, and retransmissions can slow down data transfer.
2. **Latency Issues:** Retransmissions due to errors or congestion can cause delays in data delivery.
3. **Resource Intensive:** Consumes additional processing power and memory for managing connections, flow control, and error detection.
4. **Complexity:** Transport layer protocols like TCP require complex mechanisms for reliable communication, making them harder to implement and maintain.
5. **Security Vulnerabilities:** Susceptible to cyber threats like spoofing and session hijacking if not properly secured.
6. **Packet Loss:** In unreliable protocols like UDP (User Datagram Protocol), data packets may be lost without recovery, affecting communication quality.

5. Session Layer (Layer 5)

The **Session Layer** is the **fifth layer** of the **OSI (Open Systems Interconnection) model**. It is responsible for establishing, maintaining, and terminating communication sessions between applications.

Functions

1. **Session Establishment, Maintenance, and Termination:** Creates a session between two devices, maintains it during data transfer, and terminates it when communication ends.
2. **Synchronization:** Inserts checkpoints in data streams, allowing communication to resume from a specific point in case of failure.
3. **Dialog Control:** Manages the direction of data flow (simplex, half-duplex, or full-duplex) between devices.

4. **Authentication and Authorization:** Verifies user identity and grants permissions for secure communication.
5. **Session Recovery:** Restores interrupted sessions using synchronization points without restarting from the beginning.

Protocols

1. **RPC (Remote Procedure Call):** Allows a program to request services from a remote system as if it were a local function.
2. **SMPP (Short Message Peer-to-Peer):** Enables communication between SMS applications and mobile networks.
3. **PAP (Password Authentication Protocol):** Used for user authentication in network services.
4. **NetBIOS (Network Basic Input/Output System):** Supports communication between computers on a local network.
5. **ADSP (AppleTalk Data Stream Protocol):** Manages session communication in AppleTalk networks.

6. Presentation Layer (Layer 6)

The Presentation Layer translates data into a format that the application layer can understand. It handles data encryption, compression, and formatting.

Functions

- **Translation:** Converts data between different encoding formats for interoperability.
- **Encryption:** Secures data by converting it into an unreadable format during transmission.
- **Compression:** Reduces the size of data for efficient transmission.

7. Application Layer (Layer 7)

The Application Layer provides network services directly to end-users and applications. It acts as an interface between the user and the network.

Functions

- **File Transfer and Management:** Enables access and management of files on remote systems.
- **Mail Services:** Supports email forwarding and storage.
- **Directory Services:** Provides global information about network resources.

2.5 ATM LAN EMULATION (LANE)

Asynchronous Transfer Mode (ATM) is a high-speed networking technology that provides efficient data transfer by using fixed-size cells. Since traditional Local Area Networks (LANs) such as Ethernet and Token Ring use variable-sized packets, ATM **LAN Emulation (LANE)** was developed to allow existing LAN-based applications to operate over an ATM network. LANE creates a **virtual LAN (VLAN)** over an ATM infrastructure, enabling systems to communicate as if they were on a conventional LAN while benefiting from ATM's high-speed switching and scalability.

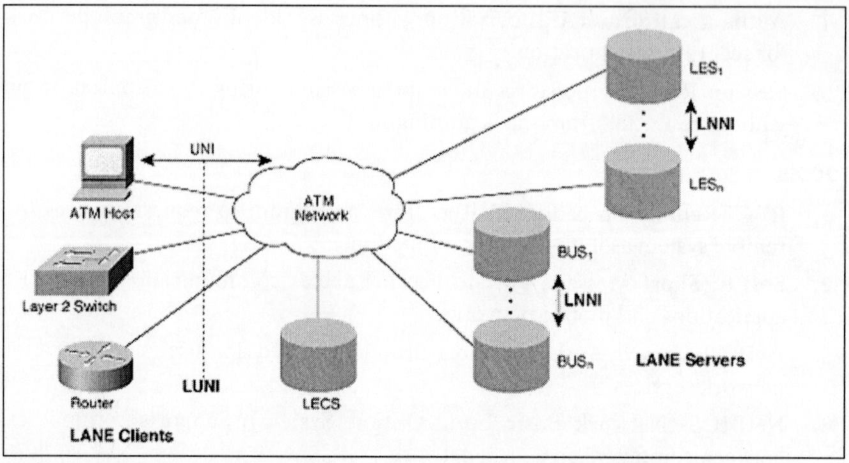

Fig. 2.9

Features of ATM LAN Emulation

1. **LAN Compatibility:** Allows Ethernet and Token Ring networks to function over ATM without modification.
2. **Address Resolution:** Maps traditional LAN addresses (MAC addresses) to ATM addresses.
3. **Virtual Circuit Establishment:** Creates logical connections between devices for efficient data transfer.
4. **Broadcast and Multicast Support:** Provides methods for forwarding broadcast and multicast traffic in an ATM environment.
5. **Quality of Service (QoS):** Offers improved traffic management with ATM's QoS capabilities.

Components of ATM LAN Emulation

1. LAN Emulation Client (LEC)

- Represents a LAN station (e.g., a computer or switch) connected to an ATM network.
- Handles communication between the traditional LAN and ATM environment.
- Sends and receives data through ATM virtual circuits.

2. LAN Emulation Server (LES)

- Manages client registrations and address lookups.
- Assists in MAC-to-ATM address resolution.

3. LAN Emulation Configuration Server (LECS)

- Provides configuration details to LECs when they join the ATM network.
- Assigns LECs to specific emulated LANs.

4. Broadcast and Unknown Server (BUS)

- Handles broadcast, multicast, and unknown traffic forwarding.
- Ensures non-ATM devices can communicate effectively in an ATM-based environment.

ATM LAN Emulation Working

1. **Client Registration:** A LAN Emulation Client (LEC) connects to the LAN Emulation Configuration Server (LECS) for configuration and assigns itself to an emulated LAN.
2. **Address Resolution:** The LEC requests the LAN Emulation Server (LES) to map MAC addresses to ATM addresses.
3. **Data Transfer:** Once address resolution is complete, the LEC establishes a direct virtual circuit to another LEC for communication.
4. **Broadcast/Multicast Handling:** If a packet needs to be sent to multiple devices, the Broadcast and Unknown Server (BUS) distributes the traffic accordingly.

2.5.1 ATM Architecture

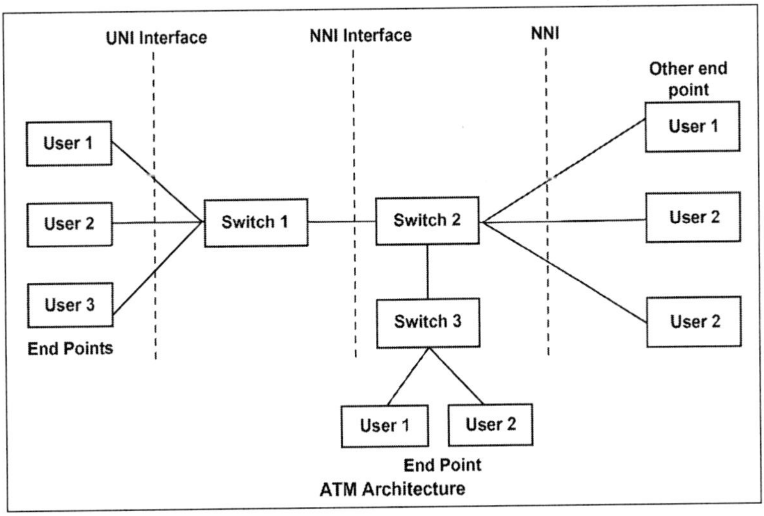

Fig. 2.10

ATM is a **connection-oriented network** where the sender or user devices, known **as end-points**, communicate over the network. These end-points connect to the network through a **User-to-Network Interface (UNI),** which links them to ATM switches. The switches, in turn, establish connections between networks using a **Network-to-Network Interface (NNI).**

ATM Transmission Path

ATM transfers data via a **transmission path** that consists **of logical virtual paths and virtual channels.** This path includes a **physical cable** that connects to an ATM switch. The cables, particularly optical fiber links, can support data transfer speeds of up to **155 megabits per second**.

Virtual Path (VP)

A transmission path is logically divided into multiple **virtual paths**, which are identified using the **Virtual Path Identifier (VPI)** within the ATM header. These virtual paths enable efficient data routing and management.

Virtual Channel (VC)

Each virtual path is further split into **virtual channels**, allowing multiple communication streams to share the same path. Every virtual channel is assigned a unique **Virtual Channel Identifier (VCI)** in the ATM header, ensuring organized data transmission across the network.

2.5.2 ATM Protocol Architecture

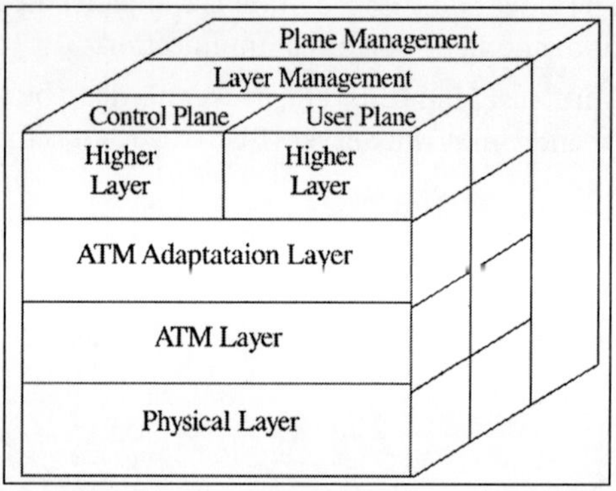

Fig. 2.11

ATM Adaptation Layer (AAL)

The **ATM Adaptation Layer (AAL)** serves as an intermediary between upper-layer protocols and ATM processes. Its primary function is to prepare user data for transmission by converting it into **48-byte cell payloads**. The AAL protocol accepts transmissions from higher-layer services and assists in mapping various applications, such as **voice and data**, to ATM cells.

Physical Layer

The Physical Layer is responsible for managing the transmission medium and is divided into two sublayers:

1. **Physical Medium-Dependent Sublayer (PMD):** Handles the physical transmission of bits over different types of media.
2. **Transmission Convergence Sublayer (TC):** Manages synchronization and ensures data integrity.

The key functions of the Physical Layer include:

- Converting **ATM cells** into a continuous bitstream.
- Controlling the **transmission and reception** of bits over the medium.
- Identifying **ATM cell boundaries** within the bitstream.
- Encapsulating **ATM cells into appropriate frames** for transmission.

ATM Layer

The **ATM Layer** is responsible for critical functions such as **cell transmission, switching, congestion control, and cell header processing**. It ensures **sequential delivery of cells** and enables multiple virtual circuits to share the same physical link, a process known as **cell multiplexing.** Additionally, it facilitates **cell relay,** which involves forwarding ATM cells across a network using **Virtual Path Identifiers (VPI)** and **Virtual Channel Identifiers (VCI)** found in the cell header.

Applications of ATM

1. ATM in Wide Area Networks (WANs)

ATM technology is widely used in **WANs** for transmitting data over long distances. It enables seamless integration with other networks through **routers**, which act as endpoints between the ATM network and external communication systems.

2. Multimedia Virtual Private Networks (VPNs) and Managed Services

ATM plays a crucial role in managing **LAN, voice, and video services** within an enterprise. It supports **full-service virtual private networking**, allowing businesses to integrate **multimedia services** efficiently.

3. Frame Relay Backbone

ATM provides a robust infrastructure for **frame relay networks**, enabling seamless internetworking between **frame relay and ATM services.** It enhances data transmission by leveraging the strengths of both technologies.

4. Residential Broadband Networks

ATM serves as a preferred choice for **residential broadband services**, offering a highly **scalable and efficient networking infrastructure** to support high-speed data, voice, and video applications.

5. Carrier Infrastructure for Telephone and Private Line Networks

Telecommunication providers utilize ATM to **optimize SONET/SDH fiber infrastructures.** It enables efficient transmission of **telephone and private-line traffic**, ensuring better resource utilization and improved network performance.

2.5.3 Token Ring

A **Token Ring network is a local area network (LAN) protocol** that operates using a ring topology. It was originally developed by **IBM** and later standardized as **IEEE 802.5**. Unlike **Ethernet,** which uses a **collision detection** mechanism, Token Ring employs a **token-passing** protocol to manage data transmission efficiently. Token ring have the following components:

1. **Token:** A small control packet that grants permission for data transmission.
2. **Stations (Nodes):** Computers or devices connected to the network.
3. **Ring Topology:** The logical structure through which data circulates in a loop.
4. **Multistation Access Unit (MAU):** A hub-like device that manages connections in modern Token Ring networks.

5. **Frame Format:** A structured data packet that includes fields such as the start delimiter, frame control, address, data, and cyclic redundancy check (CRC) for error detection.

Token Ring Working

In a **Token Ring network**, devices (computers or nodes) are arranged in a **logical ring**. A special data packet, known as a **token**, circulates continuously within the network. Devices can only transmit data when they possess the token, which prevents data collisions and ensures smooth communication.

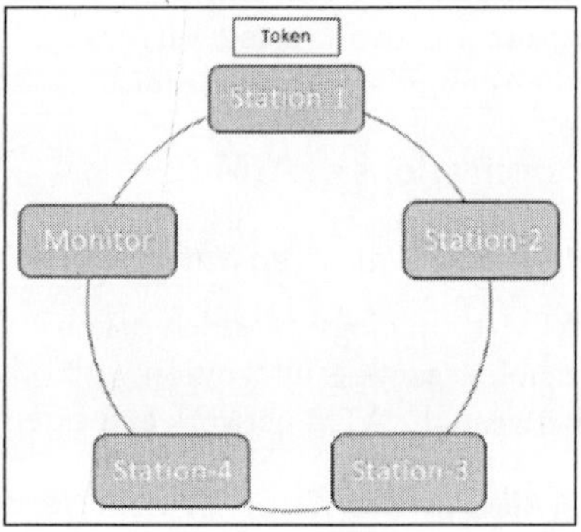

Fig. 2.12

The process involves the following steps:

1. **Token Circulation:** A free token continuously moves across the network.
2. **Data Transmission:** A device that wants to send data waits for the token, captures it, and attaches its data.
3. **Data Propagation:** The data is transmitted from one node to another along the ring until it reaches the intended recipient.
4. **Acknowledgment and Token Release:** The recipient receives the data, verifies its integrity, and sends an acknowledgment. The token is then released back into the network for the next device to use.

Token Ring Frame Structure

A Token Ring frame consists of the following key fields:

- **Start Delimiter (SD):** Marks the beginning of the frame.
- **Access Control (AC):** Indicates priority and token control information.
- **Frame Control (FC):** Specifies the type of frame being sent (data or control frame).
- **Destination Address (DA):** The address of the receiving device.
- **Source Address (SA):** The address of the sending device.
- **Data:** The actual message being transmitted.
- **Frame Check Sequence (FCS):** A checksum used for error detection.
- **End Delimiter (ED):** Marks the end of the frame.

Performance metrics determine the efficiency of networks, including **Ring Latency, ETR (Effective Transmission Rate), and DTR (Data Transfer Rate).**

1. Ring Latency

Ring Latency refers to the time it takes for a data frame or token to complete one full cycle around the ring. It includes:

- **Propagation delay** (time taken for signals to travel through cables and nodes).
- **Processing delay** (time taken by each node to read, modify, or retransmit the token or frame).
- **Queuing delay** (time spent waiting if the network is busy).

The formula for Ring Latency can be represented as:

Ring Latency = Number of Stations × Processing Time per Station + Transmission Time per Frame

A **higher ring latency** can slow down network performance, as it delays the availability of the token for other nodes.

2. ETR (Effective Transmission Rate)

ETR (Effective Transmission Rate) is the actual data rate experienced by users in a Token Ring network. It depends on multiple factors, including:

- The number of active stations.
- Network congestion and token wait times.
- Frame size and retransmission overhead.

ETR is generally lower than the theoretical data rate due to **token-passing delays, network overhead, and latency.**

3. DTR (Data Transfer Rate)

DTR (Data Transfer Rate) is the maximum **raw data rate** supported by the Token Ring network. It represents the **ideal speed** at which data could be transferred if there were no delays or overhead.

Common DTR values for Token Ring networks include:

- **4 Mbps** (Older IBM Token Ring standard).
- **16 Mbps** (IEEE 802.5 standard).
- **100 Mbps** (High-speed Token Ring, later replaced by Ethernet).

Advantages of Token Ring

1. **Collision-Free Communication:** Only one device can transmit at a time, reducing the chances of data collisions.
2. **Efficient Bandwidth Usage:** The token-passing mechanism ensures that all devices get a fair opportunity to communicate.
3. **Better Performance Under Load:** Unlike Ethernet, which can experience congestion, Token Ring maintains performance as the number of connected devices increases.
4. **Error Detection and Correction:** The network includes built-in mechanisms for identifying and correcting transmission errors.

Disadvantages of Token Ring

1. **Slower Than Ethernet:** Due to token-passing delays, it is generally slower compared to modern **Ethernet networks**.
2. **Complex Setup and Maintenance:** The network requires specialized hardware and software, making it more challenging to manage.
3. **Single Point of Failure:** If a **single device** or connection fails, the entire network may be disrupted unless redundancy mechanisms are implemented.
4. **Expensive:** Token Ring hardware is costlier than Ethernet components, leading to **higher implementation costs.**

Applications of Token Ring

- **Corporate LANs:** Used in offices and organizations where reliable and collision-free communication is needed.
- **Industrial Networks:** Found in manufacturing and automation systems for seamless data exchange.
- **Banking and Financial Institutions:** Employed to ensure secure and consistent data transmission.

2.6 INTER-LAN SWITCHING

Inter-LAN switching refers to the process of connecting multiple Local Area Networks (LANs) using network switches to enable efficient and seamless communication between devices across these networks. Switches are key networking devices that operate at the **Data Link Layer (Layer 2)** of the OSI model and are designed to forward data frames based on MAC addresses. Inter-LAN switching enhances network performance, reduces congestion, and improves scalability.

2.6.1 Types of Switches

1. Unmanaged Switches

- These are basic, plug-and-play switches with no configuration options. They are pre-configured and operate automatically.
- Ideal for small networks, home offices, or environments where simplicity and cost-effectiveness are priorities.
- **Advantages:** Easy to set up, affordable, and low maintenance.
- **Limitations:** Lack advanced features like VLANs, QoS, or security controls.

2. Managed Switches

- switches offer advanced features and can be configured and monitored by network administrators. They provide greater control over network traffic and performance.
- Suitable for medium to large networks, such as enterprise networks, data centers, and campus networks.

Advantages

- Support VLANs, QoS, and STP (Spanning Tree Protocol).
- Provide enhanced security features like MAC address filtering and access control.
- Allow remote management and monitoring.
- **Limitations:** More expensive and complex to configure than unmanaged switches.

3. Layer 2 Switches

- Operate at the Data Link Layer (Layer 2) of the OSI model and forward data frames based on MAC addresses.
- Commonly used in LANs for intra-network communication.
- Advantages: Efficiently reduce network congestion by forwarding frames only to the intended device.

- **Limitations:** Cannot route traffic between different networks (requires a Layer 3 switch or router).

4. Layer 3 Switches

- Combine the functionality of switches and routers. They operate at both the Data Link Layer (Layer 2) and the Network Layer (Layer 3), enabling them to forward data based on MAC and IP addresses.
- Ideal for inter-VLAN routing, enterprise networks, and large-scale networks.

Advantages

- Provide routing capabilities without the need for a separate router.
- Improve network performance by reducing latency.
- **Limitations:** More expensive and complex than Layer 2 switches.

5. PoE (Power over Ethernet) Switches

- These switches deliver both data and electrical power over Ethernet cables to connected devices, such as IP cameras, VoIP phones, and wireless access points.
- Commonly used in security systems, VoIP networks, and wireless deployments.

Advantages

- Eliminate the need for separate power sources for connected devices.
- Simplify installation and reduce cable clutter.
- **Limitations:** Higher cost compared to non-PoE switches.

6. Smart Switches

- Also known as "web-managed switches," these are a middle ground between unmanaged and fully managed switches. They offer limited configuration options through a web interface.
- Suitable for small to medium-sized businesses that need basic management features without the complexity of fully managed switches.

Advantages

- Provide some advanced features like VLANs and QoS.
- Easier to configure than fully managed switches.
- **Limitations:** Lack the full functionality and flexibility of managed switches.

7. Stackable Switches

- These switches can be interconnected and managed as a single unit, simplifying network management and increasing scalability.
- Ideal for growing networks that require high availability and redundancy.

Advantages

- Simplify management by treating multiple switches as one.
- Provide redundancy and failover capabilities.
- **Limitations:** Higher initial cost and complexity.

8. Modular Switches

- These switches have a chassis that allows for the addition of various modules, such as power supplies, cooling fans, and network interfaces, to meet specific needs.
- Used in large enterprises, data centers, and service provider networks.

Advantages

- Highly customizable and scalable.
- Provide flexibility to adapt to changing network requirements.
- **Limitations:** Expensive and require careful planning.

9. Fixed Configuration Switches

- These switches have a set number of ports and cannot be expanded. They are available in various port densities (e.g., 8, 24, or 48 ports).
- Suitable for small to medium-sized networks with predictable growth.

Advantages

- Cost-effective and easy to deploy.
- Available in both managed and unmanaged variants.
- **Limitations:** Lack scalability for large networks.

10. Industrial Switches

- Designed to operate in harsh environments, such as factories, outdoor locations, or areas with extreme temperatures.
- Used in industrial automation, transportation, and utility networks.

Advantages

- Rugged design with enhanced durability.
- Support for industrial protocols and standards.
- **Limitations:** Higher cost compared to standard switches.

2.6.3 Different Ways to Connect Switches

Connecting switches is a fundamental aspect of building and expanding networks. The method of connecting switches depends on the network's size, topology, and performance requirements

1. Daisy-Chaining

- In this method, switches are connected in a linear sequence, where each switch is linked to the next one in a chain-like fashion.
- It goes well with Small networks or temporary setups.

Advantages

- Simple to set up and requires minimal cabling.
- Cost-effective for small networks.

Disadvantages

- A failure in one switch can disrupt the entire chain.
- Increased latency as data passes through multiple switches.

2. Star Topology

- In a star topology, all switches are connected to a central switch or hub, forming a star-like structure.
- Each switch connects directly to the central switch, which acts as the core of the network.
- It is established in Small to medium-sized networks, such as office or campus networks.

Advantages

- Easy to manage and troubleshoot.
- Failure of one switch does not affect the others.

Disadvantages

- The central switch becomes a single point of failure.
- Requires more cabling compared to daisy-chaining.

3. Ring Topology

- In a ring topology, switches are connected in a closed loop, where each switch is linked to two others, forming a ring.
- Data travels around the ring in one direction, passing through each switch until it reaches its destination.
- It works well in the places where Networks requiring redundancy, such as industrial or control systems.

Advantages

- Redundant paths provide fault tolerance.
- Efficient for small to medium networks.

Disadvantages

- A failure in one switch or link can disrupt the entire ring.
- Complex to troubleshoot and reconfigure.

4. Mesh Topology

- In a mesh topology, every switch is connected to every other switch, creating multiple paths for data transmission.
- Switches are interconnected in a fully or partially meshed manner, ensuring multiple routes for data.
- Large networks requiring high reliability, such as data centers or enterprise networks can hold this model.

Advantages

- High redundancy and fault tolerance.
- Improved performance and load balancing.

Disadvantages

- Expensive due to the high number of connections and cables.
- Complex to set up and manage.

5. Cascading

- Cascading involves connecting switches in a hierarchical manner, where one switch serves as the main switch and others are connected to it in layers.
- The main switch connects to secondary switches, which may further connect to tertiary switches, forming a tree-like structure.
- Medium to large networks, such as campus or enterprise networks will prefer this arrangement.

Advantages

- Scalable and suitable for expanding networks.
- Reduces the load on the main switch by distributing traffic.

Disadvantages

- Increased latency for devices connected to lower-level switches.
- Requires careful planning to avoid bottlenecks.

6. Stacking

- Stacking involves connecting multiple switches using special stacking cables or ports, allowing them to operate as a single logical switch.
- Stackable switches are physically connected and managed as a unified system, sharing resources and configurations.
- It would be well suited at Networks requiring high performance and scalability, such as data centers or enterprise networks.

Advantages

- Simplified management and configuration.
- Increased bandwidth and redundancy.
- Scalable without adding complexity.

Disadvantages

- Requires compatible stackable switches.
- Higher initial cost.

7. Link Aggregation (LACP)

- Link Aggregation combines multiple physical links between switches into a single logical link to increase bandwidth and provide redundancy.

- Protocols like LACP (Link Aggregation Control Protocol) bundle multiple Ethernet links, allowing them to act as one.
- It can be relied at Networks requiring high bandwidth and reliability, such as data centers or server farms.

Advantages

- Increased bandwidth and load balancing.
- Improved fault tolerance.

Disadvantages

- Requires switches that support link aggregation.
- Slightly more complex to configure.

8. Trunking (VLAN Trunking)

- Trunking allows multiple VLANs to share a single link between switches, enabling inter-VLAN communication.
- Switches use trunking protocols like IEEE 802.1Q to tag VLAN traffic, ensuring proper routing.
- It can be well fit at Networks with multiple VLANs, such as enterprise or campus networks.

Advantages

- Efficient use of network resources.
- Simplifies VLAN management across multiple switches.

Disadvantages

- Requires switches that support trunking.
- Increased complexity in configuration.

2.7 LAN TO MAIN FRAME

Mainframes are powerful computing systems designed to handle large-scale data processing and critical business applications. Connecting mainframes to external devices and networks requires specialized hardware and software to ensure reliability, security, and performance.

The **Open Systems Adapter-Express (OSA-Express)** is an integrated LAN adapter used to connect mainframes to external devices. It functions similarly to a Network Interface Card (NIC) in Windows or UNIX systems but is tailored for mainframe environments. The OSA-Express supports various protocols and operational modes, with Ethernet being the most commonly used.

2.7.1 Network Architecture for Mainframes

1. Backbone Network

- Organizations often use a **redundant backbone switch or router** to connect critical business servers to the primary network. This setup provides multiple physical paths to the backbone, ensuring high availability and fault tolerance.

- The backbone network handles high traffic density and serves as the core of the organization's IT infrastructure.

2. Backup Site

- A **backup site** is essential for maintaining business continuity during planned or unplanned outages at the production site. The backup site can take over data processing for extended periods.
- The level of service provided by the backup site depends on the cost of maintaining it versus the potential cost of failure. Larger organizations typically invest more in robust backup solutions.
- High-speed connections, often using fiber optics, link the production and backup sites.

3. Local Offices

- Offices for IT personnel, administration, and back-office services are usually located near the production site. These offices may be in the same building, campus, or nearby locations.
- High-speed connections ensure seamless communication between these offices and the mainframe.

4. Remote Sites

- Remote locations, such as branch offices, are connected to the backbone network using carrier-supplied communication lines. These lines are designed and implemented based on the organization's requirements for speed, protocol, and topology.

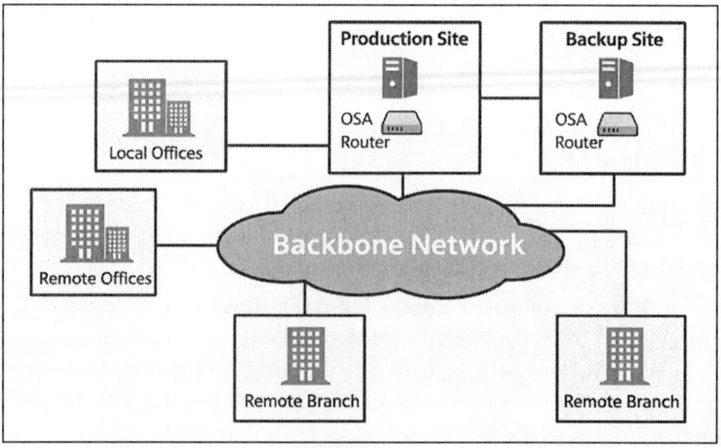

Fig. 2.13

2.7.2 Z/OS Communications Server

The **z/OS operating system** includes a software component called the **z/OS Communications Server**, which implements both **SNA (Systems Network Architecture)** and **TCP/IP protocols**. It consists of three major components:

1. TCP/IP Protocol Stack

Handles IP-based communication, enabling mainframes to connect with modern networks.

2. SNA Protocol Stack

Supports legacy mainframe communication protocols.

3. Communications Storage Manager (CSM)

Provides a shared I/O buffer area for both TCP/IP and SNA data flows, allowing host applications to share data without physically moving it.

The z/OS Communications Server enables mainframe applications to leverage advancements in communication technologies across different operating systems.

2.7.3 Security In Mainframe Networks

Mainframes are ideal for managing network transactions due to their ability to handle large volumes of data, users, and applications securely. Key security features include:

1. Physical Security

Mainframes are typically housed in secure locations with strict access controls.

2. System Authorization Facility (SAF)

SAF provides standardized authorization, authentication, and logging services. It interfaces with external security managers like **RACF (Resource Access Control Facility)** to enforce access controls.

4. Data Integrity

Mainframes ensure data integrity and reliability, even in networks supporting **thousands of users.**

2.7.4 Mainframe Network Configuration

A typical z/OS data center is structured both physically and logically:

- **Central Processor Complex (CPC):** Comprises **main storage, multiple processors, channel subsystems, and timers.**
- **Logical Partition (LPAR):** A **virtualized subset of a physical system** that operates as an independent computing environment with dedicated resources such as **processors, memory, and I/O devices.**

2.7.5 Components of the z/OS Network

1. **CICS (Customer Information Control System):** Handles **transaction processing** and enables connectivity between application programs.
2. **Coupling Facility (CF):** Facilitates **data sharing between LPARs** over high-speed channels, allowing efficient system coordination.
3. **DB2 for z/OS:** A widely used **relational database management system** (RDBMS) in enterprise mainframe environments.
4. **OSA (Open Systems Adapter):** A **high-speed network adapter** that facilitates **external communication** for the mainframe.

5. **OSPF (Open Shortest Path First):** A **routing protocol** that enables **TCP/IP traffic** between routers and the mainframe's **OMPROUTE application**.
6. **TSO (Time Sharing Option):** Allows users to establish **interactive sessions** with z/OS, similar to a command prompt in a traditional operating system.
7. **VTAM (Virtual Telecommunications Access Method):** The original **SNA protocol stack** that also supports **TCP/IP services** within z/OS.
8. **TCP/IP Server Address Spaces:** Facilitates **IP-based communication**, providing internet and intranet connectivity for the mainframe environment.

2.8 BUILDING A NETWORK

Building a network involves designing, implementing, and maintaining a system that connects devices and enables communication and resource sharing. Whether it's a small home network or a large enterprise setup, the process requires careful planning and execution.

Below are the essential steps and considerations for building a network:

1. Define Requirements

Before building a network, identify its purpose and requirements. Consider the following:

- **Scope:** Determine the size of the network (e.g., home, office, campus).
- **Users:** Estimate the number of users and devices that will connect to the network.
- **Applications:** Identify the types of applications and services the network will support (e.g., file sharing, video conferencing, cloud access).
- **Performance:** Define bandwidth, speed, and latency requirements.
- **Budget:** Establish a budget for hardware, software, and maintenance.

2. Choose the Network Type

Select the type of network based on your requirements:

- **Local Area Network (LAN):** Connects devices within a limited area, such as a home or office.
- **Wide Area Network (WAN):** Connects multiple LANs over a larger geographical area.
- **Wireless Network (Wi-Fi):** Provides wireless connectivity for devices.
- **Virtual Private Network (VPN):** Securely connects remote users to the network.

3. Design the Network Topology

The network topology defines how devices are interconnected. Common topologies include:

- **Star:** Devices connect to a central hub or switch.
- **Bus:** Devices share a single communication line.
- **Ring**: Devices are connected in a circular fashion.
- **Mesh:** Devices are interconnected, providing multiple paths for data.
- **Hybrid:** Combines two or more topologies.

Choose a topology that balances performance, scalability, and cost.

4. Select Networking Hardware

The hardware forms the backbone of the network. Key components include:

- **Routers:** Connect different networks and route data between them.
- **Switches:** Connect devices within the same network and forward data based on MAC addresses.
- **Access Points:** Provide wireless connectivity for Wi-Fi networks.
- **Network Interface Cards (NICs):** Enable devices to connect to the network.
- **Cables:** Use Ethernet cables (e.g., Cat5e, Cat6) for wired connections or fiber optics for high-speed links.
- **Firewalls:** Protect the network from unauthorized access and cyber threats.

5. Plan IP Addressing and Subnetting

Assign IP addresses to devices and divide the network into subnets for better management. Use:

- **IPv4 or IPv6**: Choose the appropriate IP version based on your needs.
- **DHCP (Dynamic Host Configuration Protocol):** Automatically assign IP addresses to devices.
- **Subnetting:** Break the network into smaller segments to improve performance and security.

6. Configure Network Protocols

Set up protocols to enable communication and data transfer:

- **TCP/IP:** The standard protocol for most networks.
- **DNS (Domain Name System):** Resolves domain names to IP addresses.
- **VLANs (Virtual LANs):** Segment the network for better traffic management and security.
- **Routing Protocols:** Use protocols like OSPF or BGP for efficient data routing.

7. Implement Security Measures

Secure the network to protect data and prevent unauthorized access:

- **Firewalls:** Monitor and control incoming and outgoing traffic.
- **Encryption:** Use protocols like WPA3 for Wi-Fi and SSL/TLS for data transmission.
- **Access Control:** Implement user authentication and authorization.
- **Regular Updates:** Keep hardware and software up to date to address vulnerabilities.

8. Test and Optimize the Network

After setting up the network, test its performance and functionality:

- **Ping and Traceroute**: Check connectivity and identify bottlenecks.
- **Bandwidth Testing:** Measure network speed and capacity.
- **Load Testing:** Simulate high traffic to ensure the network can handle peak usage.
- **Optimization**: Adjust configurations to improve performance and reliability.

9. Monitor and Maintain the Network

Regular maintenance ensures the network remains efficient and secure:

- **Monitoring Tools:** Use software to track network performance and detect issues.
- **Backups:** Regularly back up network configurations and data.
- **Troubleshooting:** Address issues promptly to minimize downtime.
- **Scalability:** Plan for future growth by ensuring the network can accommodate additional devices and users.

10. Document the Network

Maintain detailed documentation of the network setup, including:

- **Network Diagram:** Visual representation of the network topology.
- **IP Address Scheme:** List of assigned IP addresses and subnets.
- **Configuration Details:** Hardware and software configurations.
- **Security Policies:** Guidelines for network access and usage.

SUMMARY

This unit provides a comprehensive understanding of LAN connectivity for small businesses, focusing on network integration and various LAN technologies such as Token Ring, Ethernet, and ATM LAN emulation. It covers InterLAN switching to improve network performance and LAN-to-mainframe connectivity for business applications. Additionally, it explores strategies for building scalable and efficient networks, ensuring seamless communication, high-speed data transfer, and optimized resource sharing to support small business operations and growth.

EXERCISES

A. Subjective Questions

Category-I *(Revised Bloom's Levels-1, 2 & 3 – Remembering, Understanding, Applying)*

1. What are the key features of LAN connectivity in small businesses?
2. Explain the differences between Token Ring and Ethernet technologies.
3. Describe the role of ATM LAN emulation in network communication.
4. How does InterLAN Switching improve LAN performance?
5. What are the benefits of integrating LAN with mainframe systems?
6. Outline the steps involved in building a reliable LAN for a small business.
7. Define Ethernet and explain its significance in modern networks.
8. Compare and contrast LAN and WAN in terms of functionality and usage.
9. What are the key challenges in LAN-to-mainframe communication?
10. Explain the importance of network integration in small businesses.

Category-II *(Revised Bloom's Levels-4, 5 & 6 – Analyzing, Evaluating, Creating)*

1. Analyze the impact of choosing Ethernet over Token Ring in a small business environment.
2. Evaluate the effectiveness of ATM LAN emulation in improving network performance.
3. How would you design a scalable LAN for a growing business? Provide justification.
4. Assess the advantages and limitations of InterLAN Switching in a high-traffic network.
5. Propose a network integration strategy for a company transitioning from legacy systems to modern LAN technology.
6. Discuss the security implications of connecting a LAN to a mainframe system.
7. Develop a case study on a small business that successfully implemented LAN connectivity.
8. How does network redundancy play a role in building a reliable business network?
9. Critically evaluate the differences between traditional LAN technologies and modern LAN architectures.
10. What future trends do you foresee in LAN connectivity, and how can businesses prepare for them?

B. Objective Questions

Category-I *(Revised Bloom's Levels-1, 2 & 3 – Remembering, Understanding, Applying)*

1. Which of the following is a commonly used LAN technology?
   (a) Token Ring (b) SONET
   (c) DSL (d) Bluetooth
2. What is the primary function of Ethernet in a LAN?
   (a) Providing internet services
   (b) Establishing wired local network connections
   (c) Wireless communication
   (d) Data encryption
3. Which of the following is NOT a feature of LAN?
   (a) Limited geographic coverage (b) High-speed data transfer
   (c) Uses leased telecommunication lines (d) Supports multiple devices
4. Which LAN technology uses a ring topology for data transmission?
   (a) Ethernet (b) Token Ring
   (c) ATM (d) InterLAN Switching
5. ATM LAN emulation is used to:
   (a) Convert Ethernet signals into wireless signals
   (b) Provide a virtual LAN over an ATM network
   (c) Encrypt LAN communications
   (d) Replace traditional LANs

6. Which component is essential for connecting a LAN to a mainframe?
   (a) Router (b) Terminal emulator
   (c) Ethernet switch (d) Modem
7. InterLAN Switching helps in:
   (a) Increasing the number of network users
   (b) Improving LAN-to-LAN communication
   (c) Slowing down network performance
   (d) Eliminating the need for routing
8. Which of the following network technologies primarily supports small businesses?
   (a) MPLS (b) LAN
   (c) MAN (d) WAN
9. Which protocol is most commonly associated with Ethernet LANs?
   (a) IPX/SPX (b) TCP/IP
   (c) PPP (d) ATM
10. What is the primary advantage of integrating LAN with a mainframe?
    (a) Increased security vulnerabilities
    (b) Faster data access and centralized processing
    (c) Higher power consumption
    (d) More complex network setup

Ans.: 1. (a), 2. (b), 3. (c), 4. (b), 5. (b), 6. (b), 7. (b), 8. (b), 9. (b), 10. (b)

Category-II *(Revised Bloom's Levels-4, 5 & 6 – Analyzing, Evaluating, Creating)*

1. A company experiencing slow LAN performance should consider:
   (a) Ignoring the issue
   (b) Upgrading network switches and cabling
   (c) Reducing the number of network users
   (d) Removing security firewalls
2. Which factor is most critical when integrating a LAN into a growing business?
   (a) Cost-effectiveness and scalability
   (b) Using the cheapest available hardware
   (c) Limiting network expansion
   (d) Eliminating security protocols
3. A business wants to migrate from Token Ring to Ethernet. What is the biggest advantage?
   (a) Lower costs and higher speeds
   (b) Increased network complexity
   (c) Reduced compatibility with modern devices
   (d) Higher latency
4. How can a company ensure seamless LAN-to-mainframe communication?

(a) Implementing efficient terminal emulators and secure connections
(b) Removing security policies
(c) Using outdated hardware
(d) Avoiding network monitoring

5. What is the best strategy for future-proofing a small business LAN?
(a) Implementing scalable and modular network designs
(b) Relying on outdated networking technologies
(c) Avoiding security updates
(d) Using a single connection type without redundancy

6. A company is experiencing frequent network congestion. What is the best solution?
(a) Implementing VLANs and upgrading network infrastructure
(b) Reducing the number of employees using the network
(c) Ignoring the issue and hoping for improvement
(d) Switching to a flat network design

7. Which of the following is a major disadvantage of a poorly designed LAN?
(a) High-speed connectivity
(b) Network bottlenecks and security vulnerabilities
(c) Easy scalability and expansion
(d) Reduced network congestion

8. Why is InterLAN Switching crucial in a multi network environment?
(a) It simplifies connectivity between multiple LAN segments
(b) It eliminates the need for network security
(c) It slows down network communication
(d) It only benefits single-user networks

9. A business needs a high-performance network to support loud-based applications. What should they prioritize?
(a) High-speed Ethernet connections with redundancy
(b) Token Ring for backward compatibility
(c) Removing monitoring tools
(d) Ignoring network scalability

10. Which technology would best support a small business requiring high-speed LAN connections?
(a) Ethernet with Gigabit capabilities
(b) Dial-up networking
(c) Token Ring
(d) Infrared communication

Ans.: 1. (b), 2. (a), 3. (a), 4. (a), 5. (a), 6. (a), 7. (b), 8. (a), 9. (a), 10. (a)

TEACHER'S KNOW MORE

1. LAN Connectivity for Small Businesses

Small businesses rely on Local Area Networks (LANs) for efficient communication, data sharing, and resource management. A well-designed LAN improves productivity, security, and scalability. Businesses must choose the right topology and hardware based on their needs and budget.

2. Network Integration

Integration of LANs with various systems, including cloud services and mainframes, ensures seamless data flow. Proper integration strategies help businesses optimize performance, enhance security, and ensure compatibility between old and new technologies.

3. Token Ring Technology

Token Ring is a LAN technology where data travels in a circular path, reducing collisions. Though largely replaced by Ethernet due to its higher cost and complexity, it is still used in legacy systems that require deterministic network access.

4. Ethernet

Ethernet is the most widely used LAN technology, offering high-speed, low-cost, and scalable networking solutions. Variants include Fast Ethernet (100 Mbps), Gigabit Ethernet (1 Gbps), and 10-Gigabit Ethernet for high-performance networks.

5. ATM LAN Emulation

Asynchronous Transfer Mode (ATM) LAN emulation allows ATM networks to simulate traditional LAN environments. This technology was historically used to enhance speed and efficiency in large-scale enterprise networks but has declined in popularity due to the rise of Ethernet-based solutions.

6. InterLAN Switching

InterLAN Switching enables smooth communication between different LAN segments, improving traffic management and reducing network congestion. It is crucial for organizations that expand their networks and require better data flow across departments.

7. LAN to Mainframe Connectivity

Businesses with legacy mainframes must integrate LANs to ensure seamless access to centralized data and applications. This is achieved through terminal emulation, middleware solutions, and secure networking protocols like SNA (Systems Network Architecture).

8. Building Networks for Small Businesses

A well-planned network includes structured cabling, reliable hardware, scalable infrastructure, and security measures such as firewalls and encryption. Small businesses should also consider cloud networking for remote access and disaster recovery solutions.

3

UNIT

VPNs, Intranets and Extranets

RATIONALE

This unit explores virtual network management and planning, focusing on the design and implementation of VPNs for small businesses and secure remote access using IPSec VPNs. It covers strategies for integrating data centers with intranets to enhance internal communication and implementing extranets for secure external collaboration. Learners will gain practical insights into network security, scalability, and optimization, ensuring efficient and protected data exchange across distributed network environments.

UNIT OUTCOMES

- Analyze the role of VPNs, intranets, and extranets in modern network architecture and assess their effectiveness in securing communication and resource sharing.
- Design and configure VPN solutions for remote access, and develop strategies to enhance security and performance in intranet and extranet environments.

3.1 VIRTUAL NETWORK

A virtual network is a software-based representation of a physical network that enables the creation, management, and operation of network resources in a virtualized environment. It allows multiple virtual machines (VMs), containers, or devices to communicate with each other as if they were connected to a physical network, even if they are hosted on different physical servers or in different locations.

3.1.1 Key Features of Virtual Networks

- **Abstraction of Physical Infrastructure**: Virtual networks abstract the underlying physical hardware, enabling the creation of logical networks that are independent of the physical topology.
- **Isolation and Segmentation**: They provide isolated environments for different users, applications, or tenants, ensuring security and preventing interference.
- **Scalability**: Virtual networks can be easily scaled up or down to accommodate changing workloads without the need for additional physical hardware.
- **Flexibility**: They support dynamic configuration and reconfiguration, allowing administrators to adapt to changing network requirements quickly.
- **Cost Efficiency**: By reducing the need for physical hardware, virtual networks lower operational and capital expenses.

3.1.2 Types Of Virtual Networks

- **Virtual Local Area Network (VLAN)**: Segments a physical network into multiple logical networks to improve performance and security.
- **Virtual Private Network (VPN)**: Extends a private network over a public network (like the internet) to provide secure remote access.
- **Software-Defined Networking (SDN)**: Centralizes network management by separating the control plane from the data plane, enabling programmable and automated network configuration.
- **Network Function Virtualization (NFV)**: Replaces traditional network appliances (e.g., firewalls, load balancers) with virtualized software instances.

3.1.3 Applications of Virtual Networks

- **Cloud Computing**: Virtual networks are fundamental to cloud infrastructure, enabling multi-tenancy and resource sharing.
- **Data Centers**: They optimize resource utilization and simplify network management in large-scale data centers.
- **Remote Work**: VPNs facilitate secure access to corporate networks for remote employees.
- **IoT**: Virtual networks support the connectivity and management of IoT devices.

3.1.4 Benefits

- **Improved Resource Utilization**: Maximizes the use of existing hardware.
- **Enhanced Security**: Provides isolated environments and encrypted communication.
- **Simplified Management**: Centralized control and automation reduce administrative overhead.
- **Agility**: Enables rapid deployment and adaptation to new requirements.

3.1.5 Challenges

- **Performance**: Virtual networks may introduce latency or overhead compared to physical networks.
- **Complexity**: Managing virtual networks requires specialized skills and tools.
- **Security Risks**: Misconfigurations or vulnerabilities in virtualized environments can lead to breaches.

3.2 VIRTUAL NETWORK MANAGEMENT AND PLANNING

Virtual network management and planning are critical processes for ensuring the efficient, secure, and scalable operation of virtualized network environments. These processes involve designing, deploying, monitoring, and optimizing virtual networks to meet organizational requirements.

Below is a detailed description of the key aspects of virtual network management and planning:

3.2.1 Planning a Virtual Network

a. Define Objectives and Requirements

- **Business Goals**: Identify the purpose of the virtual network (e.g., supporting cloud services, enabling remote work, or hosting applications).
- **Performance Requirements**: Determine bandwidth, latency, and throughput needs.
- **Scalability**: Plan for future growth in terms of users, devices, and applications.
- **Security**: Define security policies, compliance requirements, and data protection measures.
- **Cost**: Establish a budget for hardware, software, and operational expenses.

b. Network Design

- **Topology**: Choose a network topology (e.g., hub-and-spoke, mesh, or hybrid) that aligns with the organization's needs.
- **Subnetting**: Divide the virtual network into subnets for better organization, security, and performance.
- **IP Addressing**: Plan IP address allocation, including public and private IP ranges.
- **Redundancy and High Availability**: Design failover mechanisms and redundant paths to ensure network reliability.
- **Integration with Physical Networks**: Ensure seamless connectivity between virtual and physical networks.

c. Technology Selection

- **Virtualization Platform**: Choose a hypervisor or cloud platform (e.g., VMware, Hyper-V, AWS, Azure).
- **SDN Solutions**: Consider software-defined networking (SDN) for centralized control and automation.
- **Network Appliances**: Select virtual firewalls, load balancers, and other network functions.
- **Monitoring Tools**: Identify tools for performance monitoring, troubleshooting, and analytics.

3.2.2 Deployment of Virtual Networks

a. Configuration

- **Virtual Switches and Routers**: Set up virtual switches and routers to enable communication between VMs and subnets.
- **Gateways**: Configure VPN gateways, internet gateways, or peering gateways for external connectivity.
- **Security Policies**: Implement firewalls, network security groups (NSGs), and access control lists (ACLs).
- **Network Services**: Deploy DHCP, DNS, and NAT services for IP management and address translation.

b. Testing

- **Connectivity Testing**: Verify communication between VMs, subnets, and external networks.
- **Performance Testing**: Ensure the network meets latency, bandwidth, and throughput requirements.
- **Security Testing**: Validate that security policies are enforced and vulnerabilities are addressed.

3.2.3 Virtual Network Management

a. Monitoring and Analytics

- **Traffic Monitoring**: Use tools like Wireshark, Nagios, or cloud-native monitoring solutions to track network traffic.
- **Performance Metrics**: Monitor latency, packet loss, jitter, and bandwidth utilization.
- **Logging and Auditing**: Maintain logs for troubleshooting, compliance, and security audits.

b. Automation and Orchestration

- **SDN Controllers**: Use SDN controllers to automate network configuration and management.
- **Orchestration Tools**: Leverage tools like Kubernetes, Ansible, or Terraform to manage virtual networks at scale.
- **Policy-Based Management**: Automate the enforcement of security and performance policies.

c. Security Management

- **Threat Detection**: Use intrusion detection and prevention systems (IDS/IPS) to identify and mitigate threats.
- **Encryption**: Implement encryption for data in transit (e.g., VPNs, TLS).
- **Access Control**: Regularly review and update access control policies.

d. Resource Optimization

- **Load Balancing**: Distribute traffic evenly across VMs or containers to prevent bottlenecks.
- **Capacity Planning**: Continuously assess resource usage and plan for scaling up or down.
- **Cost Management**: Optimize resource allocation to minimize costs, especially in cloud environments.

3.2.4 Maintenance and Troubleshooting

a. Regular Updates

- **Software Updates**: Keep virtualization platforms, SDN controllers, and network appliances up to date.

- **Security Patches**: Apply patches to address vulnerabilities and improve security.

b. Troubleshooting

- **Diagnostic Tools**: Use tools like ping, traceroute, and netstat to identify and resolve issues.
- **Incident Response**: Develop a plan for responding to network outages, security breaches, or performance degradation.

c. Backup and Recovery

- **Configuration Backups**: Regularly back up virtual network configurations.
- **Disaster Recovery**: Implement a disaster recovery plan to restore network operations in case of failure.

3.2.5 Scalability and Future-Proofing

a. Scalability Planning

- **Horizontal Scaling**: Add more VMs or containers to handle increased traffic.
- **Vertical Scaling**: Upgrade existing resources (e.g., CPU, memory) to improve performance.

b. Adoption of Emerging Technologies

- **5G and Edge Computing**: Plan for integration with 5G networks and edge computing infrastructure.
- **AI and Machine Learning**: Use AI-driven analytics for predictive maintenance and optimization.
- **IPv6 Adoption**: Prepare for the transition to IPv6 to address the limitations of IPv4.

3.2.6 Best Practices for Virtual Network Management and Planning

1. **Documentation**: Maintain detailed documentation of network design, configurations, and policies.
2. **Collaboration**: Involve cross-functional teams (e.g., IT, security, and operations) in planning and management.
3. **Training**: Ensure staff are trained in virtualization, SDN, and cloud networking technologies.
4. **Compliance**: Regularly audit the network to ensure compliance with industry standards and regulations.
5. **Proactive Monitoring**: Use real-time monitoring to detect and resolve issues before they impact users.

3.3 VIRTUAL NETWORK FOR A SMALL BUSINESS

Creating a virtual network for a small business involves designing a scalable, secure, and cost-effective network infrastructure that meets the business's needs. Below is a step-by-step guide along with a block diagram to illustrate the process.

3.3.1 Step-by-Step Guide to Creating a Virtual Network

1. Assess Business Requirements

- **Identify Needs**: Determine the number of users, devices, and applications that will use the network.
- **Performance Requirements**: Define bandwidth, latency, and uptime requirements.
- **Security Requirements**: Identify data protection and compliance needs.
- **Budget**: Establish a budget for hardware, software, and ongoing maintenance.

2. Choose a Virtualization Platform

- **On-Premises**: Use hypervisors like VMware ESXi, Microsoft Hyper-V, or KVM.
- **Cloud-Based**: Use cloud platforms like AWS, Microsoft Azure, or Google Cloud.
- **Hybrid**: Combine on-premises and cloud resources for flexibility.

3. Design the Network Architecture

- **Topology**: Use a hub-and-spoke or star topology for simplicity and scalability.
- **Subnets**: Divide the network into subnets for different departments (e.g., finance, HR, IT).
- **IP Addressing**: Plan IP address allocation for VMs, devices, and services.

4. Deploy Virtual Network Components

- **Virtual Switches**: Set up virtual switches to connect VMs and devices.
- **Virtual Routers**: Configure virtual routers to manage traffic between subnets and external networks.
- **Virtual Firewalls**: Implement firewalls to enforce security policies.
- **VPN Gateway**: Set up a VPN for secure remote access.

5. Configure Security

- **Network Security Groups (NSGs)**: Define rules for inbound and outbound traffic.
- **Encryption**: Use VPNs and TLS to secure data in transit.
- **Access Control**: Implement role-based access control (RBAC) for users and administrators.

6. Set Up Monitoring and Management Tools

- **Monitoring Tools**: Use tools like Nagios, PRTG, or cloud-native monitoring solutions.
- **Automation**: Use scripts or orchestration tools (e.g., Ansible, Terraform) for configuration management.

7. Test and Optimize

- **Connectivity Testing**: Verify communication between VMs, subnets, and external networks.

- **Performance Testing**: Ensure the network meets latency, bandwidth, and throughput requirements.
- **Security Testing**: Validate that security policies are enforced.

8. Train Staff

- Provide training for IT staff on managing and troubleshooting the virtual network.
- Educate employees on secure access and usage policies.

3.3.2 Block Diagram of A Virtual Network For A Small Business

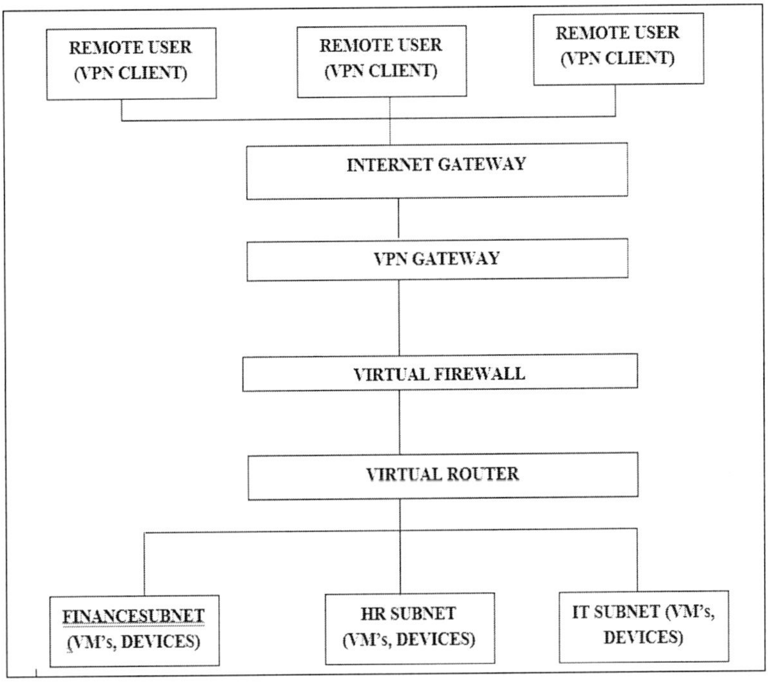

Fig. 3.1

Explanation of the Block Diagram

1. **Remote Users**: Employees access the virtual network securely via VPN clients.
2. **Internet Gateway**: Provides access to the internet for the virtual network.
3. **VPN Gateway**: Enables secure remote access to the virtual network.
4. **Virtual Firewall**: Filters traffic to enforce security policies.
5. **Virtual Router**: Manages traffic between subnets and external networks.
6. **Subnets**: Segmented networks for different departments (e.g., Finance, HR, IT).
7. **VMs and Devices**: Virtual machines and devices within each subnet.

Key Considerations for Small Businesses

1. **Scalability**: Design the network to accommodate future growth.
2. **Cost-Effectiveness**: Use open-source or cloud-based solutions to reduce costs.

3. **Security**: Implement strong encryption, access controls, and regular security audits.
4. **Ease of Management**: Use centralized management tools and automation to simplify operations.
5. **Disaster Recovery**: Implement backup and recovery plans to ensure business continuity.

3.4 SECURED REMOTE ACCESS IN VPNS

Secured remote access is a critical component of modern networking, enabling users to connect to a private network securely over the internet. Virtual Private Networks (VPNs) are the most common technology used to achieve this. They create an encrypted tunnel between the user's device and the private network, ensuring data confidentiality, integrity, and authenticity.

1. Secured Remote Access

Secured remote access allows authorized users to connect to a private network from a remote location securely. It ensures that sensitive data transmitted over the internet is protected from unauthorized access, interception, or tampering. VPNs are the primary tool for achieving secured remote access.

2. VPNs Enable Secured Remote Access

A VPN creates a secure, encrypted connection (often called a "tunnel") between the user's device and the private network. This tunnel ensures that all data transmitted between the two endpoints is encrypted and protected from eavesdropping or attacks.

3. Key Components of Secured Remote Access in VPNs

a. VPN Client

- Software installed on the user's device (e.g., laptop, smartphone, or tablet).
- Initiates the connection to the VPN server.
- **Examples:** OpenVPN, Cisco AnyConnect, FortiClient.

b. VPN Server

- A gateway that authenticates users and establishes the encrypted tunnel.
- Located within the private network or hosted in the cloud.
- **Examples:** Windows Server with VPN role, OpenVPN Access Server.

c. Encryption Protocols

- Ensure data confidentiality and integrity by encrypting traffic.
- **Common protocols:** IPsec, SSL/TLS, OpenVPN, WireGuard.

d. Authentication Mechanisms

- Verify the identity of users before granting access.
- **Methods:** Username/password, multi-factor authentication (MFA), certificates.

e. Tunneling Protocols

- Define how data is encapsulated and transmitted over the VPN.
- Examples: PPTP, L2TP, SSTP, IKEv2.

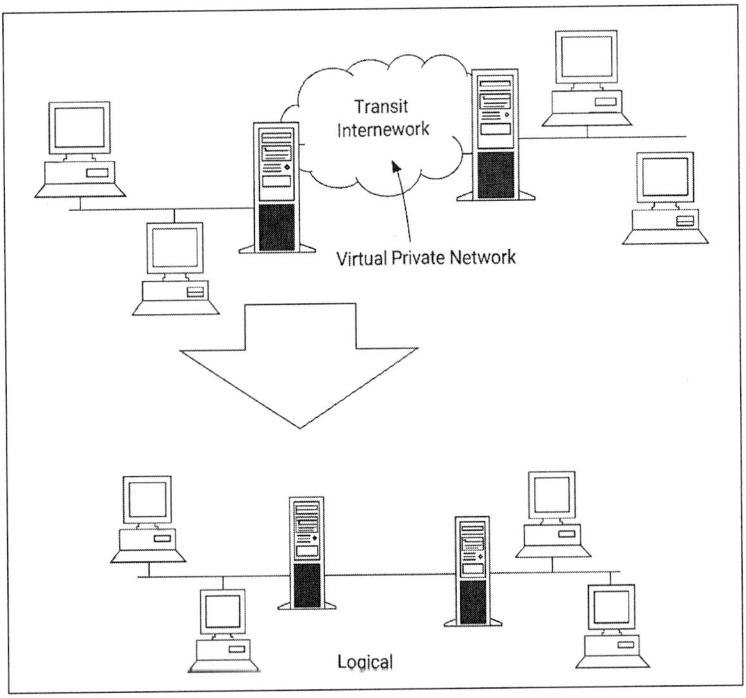

Fig. 3.2

4. VPN Protocols for Secured Remote Access

a. IPsec (Internet Protocol Security)

- **Description**: A suite of protocols for securing IP communications.
- **Features:**
  - Provides encryption and authentication.
  - Supports both transport mode (end-to-end) and tunnel mode (network-to-network).
- **Use Case**: Commonly used in site-to-site VPNs and remote access VPNs.

b. SSL/TLS (Secure Sockets Layer/Transport Layer Security)

- **Description**: Encrypts data at the application layer.
- **Features**:
  - Uses certificates for authentication.
  - Works over standard web browsers (no additional client software required).
- **Use Case**: Ideal for web-based remote access and client-to-site VPNs.

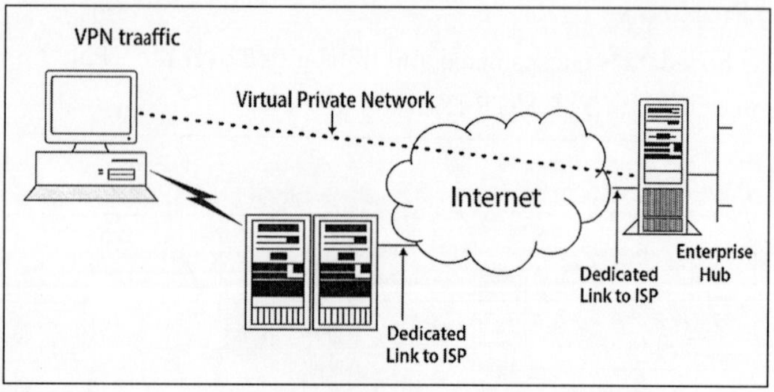

Fig. 3.3

c. OpenVPN

- **Description**: An open-source VPN protocol based on SSL/TLS.
- **Features**:
  - Highly configurable and secure.
  - Supports both UDP and TCP for flexibility.
- **Use Case**: Suitable for small businesses and individuals.

d. WireGuard

- **Description**: A modern, lightweight VPN protocol.
- **Features**:
  - Faster and simpler than traditional protocols.
  - Uses state-of-the-art cryptography.
- **Use Case**: Ideal for high-performance and low-latency applications.

e. L2TP/IPsec (Layer 2 Tunneling Protocol with IPsec)

- **Description**: Combines L2TP for tunneling and IPsec for encryption.
- **Features**:
  - Provides strong security.
  - Supported by most operating systems.
- **Use Case**: Used in remote access and site-to-site VPNs.

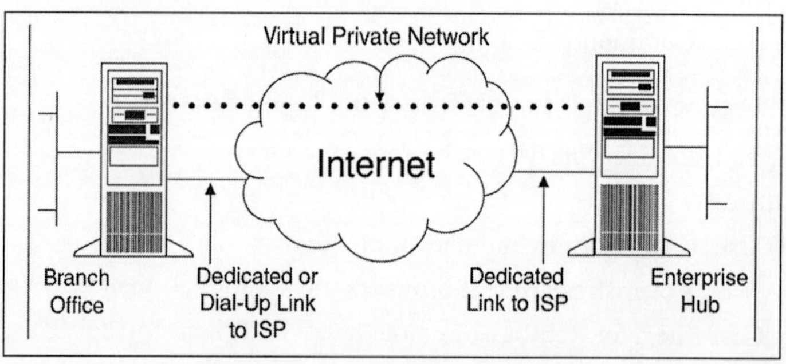

Fig. 3.4

5. Benefits of Secured Remote Access in VPNs

1. **Data Confidentiality**: Encrypts data to prevent unauthorized access.
2. **Data Integrity**: Ensures data is not tampered with during transmission.
3. **Authentication**: Verifies the identity of users and devices.
4. **Flexibility**: Enables remote work and access to resources from anywhere.
5. **Cost-Effectiveness**: Reduces the need for dedicated leased lines.

6. Challenges of Secured Remote Access in VPNs

1. **Performance Overhead**: Encryption and tunneling can introduce latency.
2. **Complexity**: Requires proper configuration and management.
3. **Security Risks**: Misconfigurations or vulnerabilities can lead to breaches.
4. **Scalability**: Supporting a large number of remote users can strain resources.

3.5 IPSEC VPN

An IPSec VPN is a virtual private network that uses the IPSec protocol suite to establish secure, encrypted connections between devices or networks over the internet. It ensures data confidentiality, integrity, and authenticity by encrypting IP packets and authenticating the communicating parties

a. Security Protocols

- **AH (Authentication Header)**:
  - Provides data integrity and authentication.
  - Does not encrypt data, so it is often used in combination with ESP.
- **ESP (Encapsulating Security Payload)**:
  - Provides data encryption, integrity, and authentication.
  - Commonly used for securing data in IPSec VPNs.

b. Encryption Algorithms

- Used by ESP to encrypt data.
- **Examples:** AES (Advanced Encryption Standard), 3DES (Triple Data Encryption Standard).

c. Authentication Methods

- Verify the identity of communicating parties.
- **Examples:** Pre-shared keys (PSK), digital certificates.

d. Key Management

- **IKE (Internet Key Exchange)**:
  - A protocol used to establish shared security attributes and keys between devices.
  - Operates in two phases:
    - **Phase 1**: Establishes a secure channel for key exchange.
    - **Phase 2**: Negotiates the encryption keys for the IPSec tunnel.

e. Security Associations (SAs)

- Define the parameters for secure communication, such as encryption algorithms and keys.
- Established during the IKE negotiation process.

3.5.1 Modes of Operation in IPSe VPNs

a. Transport Mode

- **Description**: Encrypts only the payload (data) of the IP packet, leaving the header intact.
- **Use Case**: Suitable for end-to-end communication between two devices (e.g., a client and a server).
- **Advantages**: Lower overhead, faster performance.
- **Disadvantages**: Does not protect the IP header, making it less secure for some use cases.

b. Tunnel Mode

- **Description**: Encrypts the entire IP packet (header and payload) and encapsulates it within a new IP packet.
- **Use Case**: Ideal for site-to-site VPNs, where entire networks are connected securely.
- **Advantages**: Protects the entire IP packet, including the header.
- **Disadvantages**: Higher overhead due to encapsulation.

3.5.2 IPSec VPNS Working

Step 1: Initiation

- The VPN client or gateway initiates a connection to the VPN server or peer.

Step 2: IKE Phase 1

- Establishes a secure channel for key exchange.
- Uses Diffie-Hellman key exchange to create a shared secret.
- Authenticates the parties using pre-shared keys or digital certificates.

Step 3: IKE Phase 2

- Negotiates the encryption keys and algorithms for the IPSec tunnel.
- Establishes Security Associations (SAs) for the session.

Step 4: Data Transfer

- Data is encrypted and encapsulated using ESP or AH.
- Packets are transmitted securely over the internet.

Step 5: Termination

- The VPN connection is terminated when the session ends or the SA expires.

3.5.3 Advantages of IPSec VPNS

1. **Strong Security**: Provides robust encryption, authentication, and data integrity.
2. **Interoperability**: Supported by most operating systems and network devices.
3. **Scalability**: Suitable for both small and large networks.
4. **Flexibility**: Can be used for remote access and site-to-site VPNs.
5. **Transparency**: Works at the network layer, so it is application-independent.

3.5.4 Disadvantages of IPSec VPNS

1. **Complexity**: Requires careful configuration and management.
2. **Performance Overhead**: Encryption and encapsulation can introduce latency.
3. **NAT Traversal Issues**: IPSec can have compatibility issues with NAT (Network Address Translation), though NAT-T (NAT Traversal) mitigates this.
4. **Firewall Configuration**: May require adjustments to firewall rules to allow IPSec traffic.

3.6 INTEGRATING DATA CENTERS WITH INTRANETS

Integrating data centers with intranets involves connecting the centralized computing and storage resources of a data center to an organization's private internal network (intranet). This integration enables seamless access to data, applications, and services hosted in the data center while ensuring security, performance, and scalability.

- **Data Center**: A facility that houses centralized computing resources, such as servers, storage systems, and networking equipment, to support an organization's IT operations.
- **Intranet**: A private internal network used by an organization to share information, resources, and applications securely among employees.

Purpose of Integration

Integrating data centers with intranets allows employees to access critical business applications, databases, and services hosted in the data center securely and efficiently. It ensures that resources are centralized, manageable, and accessible to authorized users within the organization. Consider the following for integration:

- **Bandwidth Requirements**: Ensure sufficient bandwidth to handle traffic between the data center and intranet.
- **Latency**: Minimize latency for real-time applications by optimizing network paths.
- **Disaster Recovery**: Implement backup and recovery plans to ensure business continuity.
- **Compliance**: Ensure the integration meets regulatory and industry standards (e.g., GDPR, HIPAA)

Key Steps for Integration

a. Network Connectivity

- Establish high-speed, reliable connections between the data center and the intranet.
- Use technologies like MPLS (Multiprotocol Label Switching), VPNs (Virtual Private Networks), or dedicated leased lines.

b. Security Measures

- Implement firewalls, intrusion detection/prevention systems (IDS/IPS), and encryption to protect data in transit.
- Use access control mechanisms like role-based access control (RBAC) to restrict access to sensitive resources.

c. Load Balancing

- Deploy load balancers to distribute traffic evenly across servers in the data center, ensuring optimal performance and availability.

d. Centralized Authentication

- Use directory services like Active Directory (AD) or LDAP (Lightweight Directory Access Protocol) to manage user authentication and authorization across the intranet and data center.

e. Application Integration

- Ensure that applications hosted in the data center are accessible via the intranet.
- Use APIs (Application Programming Interfaces) or web services to enable seamless communication between applications.

f. Monitoring and Management

- Implement network monitoring tools to track performance, detect issues, and ensure uptime.
- Use centralized management platforms to oversee both the data center and intranet resources.

Benefits of Integration

1. **Centralized Resource Management**: Simplifies the management of IT resources by consolidating them in the data center.
2. **Improved Accessibility**: Employees can access data and applications from anywhere within the intranet.
3. **Enhanced Security**: Centralized security measures protect sensitive data and resources.
4. **Scalability**: Easily scale resources in the data center to meet growing demands.
5. **Cost Efficiency**: Reduces the need for redundant infrastructure and lowers operational costs.

Use Cases

1. **Enterprise Applications**: Hosting ERP, CRM, and other business-critical applications in the data center for intranet access.
2. **Collaboration Tools**: Providing access to tools like SharePoint or intranet portals.
3. **Data Storage and Backup**: Centralizing data storage and backup solutions in the data center.

3.7 IMPLEMENTING AND SUPPORTING EXTRANETS

An **extranet** is a secure, private network that enables authorized external users, such as suppliers, clients, and business partners, to access an organization's resources. It serves as a controlled communication channel between a company and external stakeholders, ensuring secure information exchange. Access is typically granted through authentication mechanisms like usernames and passwords. The extranet functions as an extension of an organization's intranet, with firewall protection to ensure security and restricted access.

Examples of Extranet Usage

1. **E-commerce Platforms:** Online businesses use extranets to share data with suppliers and retailers, improving inventory and order management.
2. **Corporate Collaboration:** Large organizations utilize extranets to manage projects, communicate with clients, and coordinate with partner companies.
3. **Educational Institutions:** Universities provide e-learning portals to students through an extranet, allowing access to academic resources from anywhere.

Implementation of Extranet

Extranets are primarily set up using a **Virtual Private Network (VPN)** to establish a secure communication channel between organizations. A VPN encrypts data transmitted over a public network like the internet, ensuring privacy and security.

Role of IPsec in Extranet Security

Internet Protocol Security (IPsec) is a key component of VPNs that adds an additional security layer to the standard **Transmission Control Protocol/Internet Protocol** (TCP IP).

IPsec Tunneling Provides

- **Privacy:** Ensures confidential data transmission between authorized users.
- **Integrity:** Protects against data alteration and ensures secure data exchange.
- **Authentication:** Grants access only to verified users.

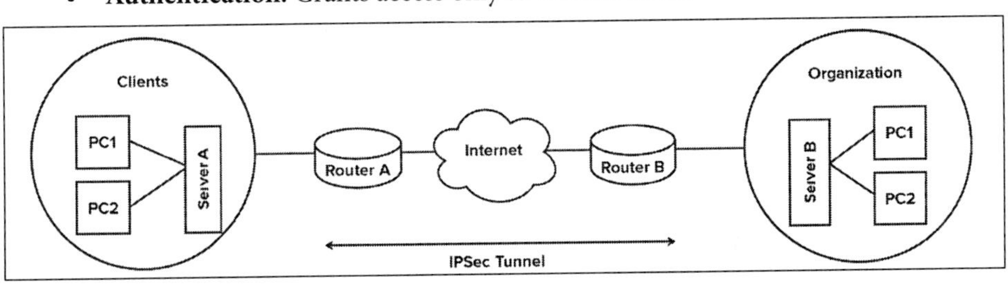

Fig. 3.5

IPsec Protocols Used in Extranets

There are two primary security protocols used in an extranet network:

1. **Authentication Header (AH):** Focuses on authentication and data integrity but does not encrypt data. It verifies the source and prevents tampering.
2. **Encapsulating Security Payload (ESP):** Provides encryption, authentication, integrity, and anti-replay protection. It ensures secure communication by either encrypting the data, authenticating it, or both.

Features of an Extranet

1. **Secure Data Exchange:** Protects sensitive information shared between organizations, reducing risks of data breaches.
2. **Efficient Communication:** Enables real-time collaboration between multiple organizations, enhancing workflow efficiency.
3. **Scalability and Flexibility:** Provides an adaptable and expandable networking environment to meet business needs.
4. **Cost Reduction:** Minimizes expenses related to paperwork, travel, and manual communication.
5. **Authentication and Access Control:** Restricts access to authorized users through secure login credentials.

Advantages of an Extranet

- **Enhanced Security:** Utilizing VPNs ensures encrypted and secure communication between businesses.
- **High Data Transfer Capacity:** Supports large-scale data exchange between organizations while maintaining security and reliability.
- **Seamless Collaboration:** Allows multiple companies to connect and collaborate efficiently on joint projects.
- **Improved Communication:** Provides a dedicated communication channel for both internal and external users, ensuring smoother interactions.

Challenges and Limitations of an Extranet

1. Complex Security Management

- If an extranet is hosted on an internal server, additional firewalls are required, increasing management workload.

2. Hosting Requirements

- Requires **high-speed internet** for optimal performance, which may not always be available to all users.

3. Cost Considerations

- More expensive than an intranet due to additional security layers and hosting infrastructure.

4. Internet Dependency

- Since extranets operate over the internet, disruptions in connectivity can impact business operations.

Feature	Internet	Intranet	Extranet
Definition	A global network that connects millions of devices and users worldwide.	A private network used within an organization to share internal resources.	A private network that allows controlled access to external users like partners, suppliers, and clients.
Access	Open to the public; anyone can access it.	Restricted to employees or authorized personalk of an organization.	Restricted to specifie external users with authentication.
Users	General public, businesses, individuals, and organizations.	Employees and internal staff of an organization.	Selected external stakeholders such as vendors, customers, or business partners.
Security	Less secure, data is vulnerable to cyber threats.	Highly secure with restricted access and firewalls.	Secure but allows external access with authentication mechanisms.
Usage	Used for global communication, browsing, social networking, and online transactions.	Used for internal communication, file sharing, and company resource.	Used for collabration, secure data sharing, and business-to-business (B2B) communication.
Examples	Websites, emails, social media, search engines.	Internal portals, HR management systems, company policies, and knowledge bases.	Supplier portals, e-learning platforms, and secure business networks.

SUMMARY

- Virtual network management and planning are essential for building and maintaining a robust, secure, and scalable network infrastructure. By carefully design and implementation organizations can optimize performance, reduce costs, and adapt to changing business needs.
- IPSec VPNs remain a cornerstone of modern network security, offering robust protection for sensitive data in transit.
- Integrating data centers with intranets is essential for modern organizations to centralize resources, improve accessibility, and enhance security. It can create a seamless and efficient connection between their data centers and intranets, enabling employees to access critical resources securely and reliably.
- Despite challenges such as internet dependency and security management, extranets enhance collaboration, improve efficiency, and facilitate seamless business operations.

TEACHER'S KNOW MORE

- **Virtual Network Management:** Explain strategies for efficient network planning, monitoring, and scalability.
- **VPNs for Small Businesses:** Cover types, benefits, and secure deployment of VPNs for remote work.
- **Secure Remote Access & IPSec VPNs:** Teach encryption, authentication, and tunneling protocols for safe data transmission.
- **Data Center & Intranet Integration:** Explain methods to connect data centers securely with internal networks.
- **Extranet Implementation:** Discuss configuring extranets for controlled business collaboration with external partners.

EXERCISES

A. Subjective Questions

Category-I ***(Revised Bloom's Levels-1, 2 & 3 – Remembering, Understanding, Applying)***

1. Define Virtual Network Management and explain its role in modern networking.
2. What are VPNs, and why are they essential for small businesses?
3. Explain how Secure Remote Access works in a VPN.
4. Describe IPSec VPNs and their significance in network security.
5. How do data centers integrate with intranets to enhance connectivity?
6. Differentiate between an Intranet and an Extranet.
7. What are the key components required to implement an Extranet?
8. Explain the basic working principles of a VPN tunnel.
9. What are the benefits of using a VPN for remote employees?
10. How does encryption enhance VPN security?

Category-II ***(Revised Bloom's Levels-4, 5 & 6 – Analyzing, Evaluating, Creating)***

1. Analyze the impact of VPNs on cybersecurity in small businesses.
2. How would you design a secure remote access VPN for an organization with multiple locations?
3. Evaluate the advantages and disadvantages of IPSec VPNs compared to SSL VPNs.
4. Assess the challenges faced when integrating data centers with intranets.
5. Propose an effective strategy for implementing and supporting an extranet for business partners.
6. How would you troubleshoot connectivity issues in a VPN setup?
7. Compare the security features of different types of VPNs used in business environments.
8. If a company is experiencing slow VPN performance, what steps can be taken to optimize it?

9. Discuss the role of firewalls and network policies in securing a VPN infrastructure.
10. Design a scalable VPN solution for a growing business that requires secure access for remote employees and third-party vendors.

B. Objective Questions

Category-I ***(Revised Bloom's Levels-1, 2 & 3 – Remembering, Understanding, Applying)***

1. Which of the following best describes a Virtual Private Network (VPN)?
   (a) A network that uses private IP addresses only
   (b) A secure tunnel between networks over the internet
   (c) A replacement for physical network connections
   (d) A protocol used for wireless networks
2. What is the primary purpose of a VPN in a business environment?
   (a) To increase internet speed
   (b) To enable secure remote access to company resources
   (c) To replace LAN infrastructure
   (d) To provide free internet access
3. Which protocol is commonly used for secure VPN connections?
   (a) FTP (b) IPSec
   (c) SMTP (d) HTTP
4. What does IPSec stand for?
   (a) Internet Protocol Secure
   (b) International Private Secure Connection
   (c) Internet Packet Security
   (d) Internal Privacy and Secure Communication
5. Which type of VPN is best suited for remote employees needing secure access?
   (a) Site-to-Site VPN (b) Remote Access VPN
   (c) Intranet VPN (d) Extranet VPN
6. Which encryption method is commonly used in VPNs?
   (a) AES (b) MD5
   (c) Telnet (d) POP3
7. Which of the following is a key feature of an Extranet?
   (a) It is restricted to employees only
   (b) It allows secure communication with external users
   (c) It is not accessible from outside the organization
   (d) It does not require authentication

8. What is the main function of a VPN tunnel?
   (a) To increase network bandwidth
   (b) To secure data transmission over public networks
   (c) To bypass network firewalls
   (d) To provide free internet access
9. Which VPN technology is best for encrypting traffic at the IP layer?
   (a) SSL VPN (b) IPSec VPN
   (c) GRE Tunnel (d) L2TP VPN
10. What is a key advantage of integrating data centers with intranets?
   (a) Faster internet speed
   (b) Secure internal data sharing and management
   (c) Reduced need for VPNs
   (d) Eliminates network security risks

Ans.: 1. (b), 2. (b), 3. (b), 4. (a), 5. (b), 6. (a), 7. (b), 8. (b), 9. (b), 10. (b)

4

UNIT

Networking Tools and Simulation

RATIONALE

This unit explores simulation methods for designing efficient multimedia networks, focusing on predicting performance, optimizing traffic flow, and ensuring reliability. It covers techniques for determining remote bridge and router delays, helping to minimize latency and improve data transmission. Also emphasizes network baselining as a critical planning tool for performance assessment and future expansion. Learners will gain insights into network optimization strategies for enhanced scalability, security, and efficiency in multimedia communications.

OUTCOME

- Understand the role of simulation techniques in designing multimedia networks and evaluate their effectiveness in predicting performance metrics such as bandwidth, latency, and traffic flow.
- Determine remote bridge and router delays, and utilize network baselining as a strategic planning tool to enhance reliability, efficiency, and scalability in multimedia network deployments.

4.1 INTRODUCTION TO MULTIMEDIA

Multimedia is uses more than one media element. Web-based multimedia provides interactive experience which incorporates two or more media elements such as text, graphics, sound, animation and video. Web-based multimedia provides interactivity which is more important in various applications like World Wide Web, Multimedia Authoring, Adobe-Macromedia Director, Hypermedia courseware and Video. Examples: Interactive TV, Computer Games, Virtual reality, Digital video editing and production systems Multimedia Database system.

4.1.1 Introduction to Hypertext and Hypermedia

Hypertext is a text which contains links to other texts. The term was invented by Ted Nelson around 1965. HyperText Navigation is traversal through pages of hypertext which is non-linear. HyperMedia is not constrained to be text-based. It includes other media, e.g., graphics, images, and especially the continuous media – sound and video. The World Wide Web (WWW) is the best example of a hypermedia application. The other examples are Powerpoint, Adobe Acrobat (or other PDF software) and Adobe Flash.

4.1.2 Categories of Multimedia Applications

A multimedia website can be linear, which users start at the beginning and progress through a set sequence of events until they reach the end. But most websites use a nonlinear approach to navigation, which users have more control over what they are interested in pursuing. It enables the user to directly respond to and control any or all of the media elements. Hence, users of interactive multimedia applications become active participants instead of the passive recipients of information.

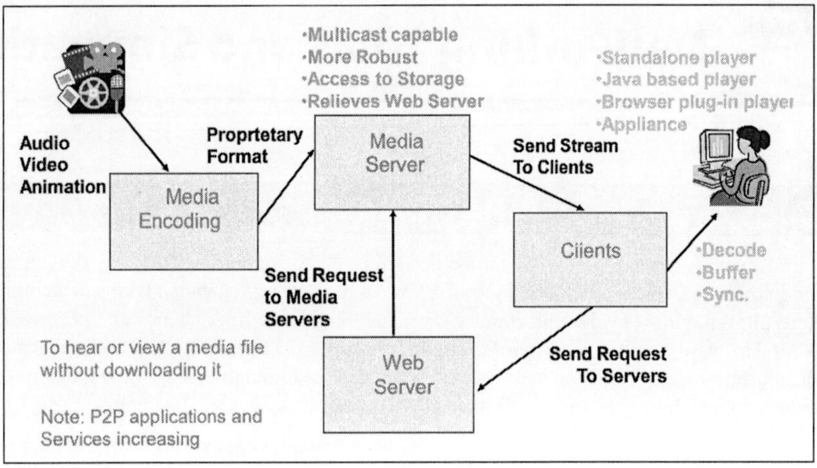

Fig. 4.1

4.1.3 Benefits of Multimedia

- Provides an excellent way to convey content
- Uses a variety of media elements to reinforce one idea
- Activates multiple senses creating rich experiences
- Gives life to flat information
- Enhances user enjoyment
- Improves retention
- Enables users to control Web experience
- Addresses multiple learning styles

4.1.4 Applications of Multimedia

Multimedia in Business

Business application that are multimedia based include presentations, training, marketing, advertising, product demos, databases, catalogues, and networked communications. Multimedia is getting much utilization in training programs.

Multimedia in School

Schools are perhaps the most ideal target for multimedia. Its rich set of media is potential for delivering effective teaching. Multimedia equipped education lets the students. Learn at their own pace and at their own time. It is ideal in distance education and open learning systems wherein students need not to be physically present in class. Students can learn while having fun.

Multimedia at Home

From cooking to gardening, home design to repair, indeed multimedia has made itself useful at home. It enables you to convert your video to digital format, store your pictures in a compact disc, and many more. Today, multimedia is also being applied in our TV and soon, multimedia projects will reach out homes via interactive TV (iTV).

Multimedia in Public Places

Multimedia is present in standalone terminals, or kiosks, in airport terminals, hotels, mall, train stations, museums, grocery stores, and more. It provides us information and help about a particular place. Interactive kiosks enables you to make a transaction without talking to a sales agent.

Multimedia in the Internet

Multimedia was introduced in the Internet with the advent of the WWW. In fact, the Web is the multimedia part of the internet. In the early stages of the internet, you can view information in plain text. The Web enables multimedia to be delivered online. Playing live Internet games with multiple players around the world has caught much attention. Some e-learning systems use multimedia on the internet as a method to deliver learning materials to students anywhere.

Multimedia in Mobile Devices

Mobile devices such as personal digital assistants (PDAs or handheld computers), smartphones, and mobile devices are not exceptions to multimedia. MMS (Multimedia Messages Services) is a store-and-forward method of transmitting graphics, video clips, sound files, and short text messages over wireless network using the WAP. It also supports email addressing, so the device can send-emails directly to communication between mobile phones

4.1.5 Multimedia Expectations from Communication Network

The various requirements are traffic requirement and functional requirements.

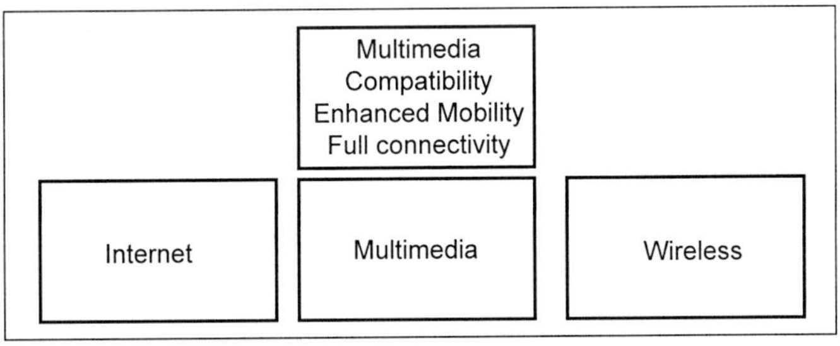

Fig. 4.2

Traffic Requirements

- Limits on real time parameters like delay and jitter
- Bandwidth and reliability
- Synchronization

Functional Requirements

- Support for multimedia services such as multicasting, security, mobility and session management.
- Supporting multimedia applications over computer network renders the application distributed. Multimedia transmission takes place over wireless and wired networks.

4.1.6 Problems in Multimedia Expectations

Multimedia Data is Large in Size

Wireless/Internet lacks guarantee to performance due to lack of self QoS provision, packet loss, Congestion, latency, delay jitters, errors in wireless links.

Internet is heterogeneous due to varying network conditions, user preferences and device capabilities

Solution

End System Based

1. **Compression:** This is achieved by way of layered and scalable coding. The layers possible are base layer and enhancement layers. The coding include MPEG Scalable Video Coding(SVC), MPEG(using spatial and temporal scalability) and MPEG-4 (Fine granularity scalability-FGS & H.264)
2. Media distribution
3. Media Synchronization
4. Media network protocol
5. **End System Based:** This includes QoS control. The QoS control deals with congestion control and error control. Source-based rate control, receiver based rate control and hybrid rate control. The various error control are FEC, retransmission(ARQ), error resilient encoding and error concealment.

Network Centric Based

1. **Packet Classification:** Packet is based on type of service
2. **Packet Scheduling:** The packets to send are chosen in order
3. **Integrated services:** The flow based architecture for providing QoS guarantees in P network for individual application
4. **Differentiated services are packet based:** The IP packet is marked to specify the treatment.
5. Multiprotocol label switching which combines both flow and packet based. The forwarding scheme tags packets with labels.

4.1.7 Introduction to Network Modeling

Network modeling is the process of creating a simplified representation of a network to analyze its behavior, performance, and efficiency. It is a critical step in designing, optimizing, and troubleshooting networks, as it allows engineers to predict how a network will perform under various conditions without physical deployment. Network models are used in areas such as capacity planning, protocol design, QoS evaluation, and security analysis.

Objectives of Network Modeling

- **Performance Analysis:** Evaluate how the network performs under different traffic loads and configurations.
- **Resource Optimization:** Identify the most efficient use of network resources, such as bandwidth, routers, and switches.
- **Fault Tolerance:** Test the network's ability to handle failures or unexpected events.
- **Scalability Testing:** Assess how the network can grow to accommodate more users or devices.
- **Cost Estimation:** Estimate the costs associated with deploying and maintaining the network.

Key Components of Network Modeling

- **Network Topology:** The physical or logical layout of the network, including nodes (e.g., routers, switches, servers) and links (e.g., wired or wireless connections).
- **Traffic Models:** Representations of data flow within the network, such as voice, video, or file transfer traffic. Common models include Poisson, Markov, and self-similar traffic.
- **Protocols:** The rules and standards governing data communication, such as TCP/IP, UDP, or HTTP.
- **Performance Metrics:** Key indicators of network performance, such as latency, throughput, packet loss, and jitter.
- **Resource Constraints:** Limitations on network resources, such as bandwidth, buffer size, or processing power.

Steps in the Network Modeling Process

- **Step 1:** Define Objectives
  - Clearly outline the goals of the modeling process, such as evaluating QoS, testing scalability, or optimizing resource allocation.
- **Step 2:** Gather Requirements
  - Collect information about the network's purpose, expected traffic patterns, user requirements, and performance goals.
- **Step 3:** Design the Network Topology
  - Create a representation of the network's structure, including nodes, links, and routing paths. Common topologies include star, mesh, ring, and tree.
- **Step 4:** Select Traffic Models
  - Choose appropriate models to simulate the behavior of different types of traffic, such as voice, video, or data.
- **Step 5:** Configure Protocols and Parameters
  - Define the protocols to be used and set parameters such as packet size, transmission rates, and error rates.

- **Step 6:** Implement the Model
  - Use simulation tools (e.g., NS-3, OMNeT++, OPNET) or mathematical models to implement the network design.
- **Step 7:** Run Simulations
  - Execute the model under various scenarios to collect data on network performance.
- **Step 8:** Analyze Results
  - Evaluate the simulation output to identify bottlenecks, inefficiencies, or areas for improvement.
- **Step 9:** Optimize and Iterate
  - Refine the network design based on the analysis and repeat the process until the desired performance is achieved.

Types of Network Models

- **Analytical Models:**
  - Use mathematical equations to represent network behavior.
  - Suitable for simple networks with well-defined traffic patterns.
  - **Examples:** Queuing theory, Markov chains.
- **Simulation Models:**
  - Use software tools to emulate network behavior in a virtual environment.
  - Suitable for complex networks with dynamic traffic and multiple protocols.
  - **Examples:** NS-3, OMNeT++, OPNET.
- **Hybrid Models:**
  - Combine analytical and simulation approaches to leverage the strengths of both methods.
  - Useful for large-scale networks with mixed traffic types.

Challenges in Network Modeling

- **Complexity:** Modeling large-scale networks with diverse traffic types and protocols can be challenging.
- **Accuracy:** Ensuring that the model accurately reflects real-world behavior requires careful calibration.
- **Scalability:** Simulating large networks can be computationally intensive and time-consuming.
- **Dynamic Traffic:** Network traffic is often unpredictable and bursty, making it difficult to model accurately.
- **Resource Constraints:** Limited computational resources can restrict the scope and detail of the model.

Applications of Network Modeling

- **Capacity Planning:** Determine the resources needed to support future network growth.

- **Protocol Design:** Test and optimize new or existing network protocols.
- **QoS Evaluation:** Ensure that the network meets performance requirements for different types of traffic.
- **Security Analysis:** Identify vulnerabilities and test the effectiveness of security measures.
- **Disaster Recovery:** Plan for network failures and ensure business continuity.

Tools for Network Modeling

- **NS-3:** An open-source network simulator for wired and wireless networks.
- **OMNeT++:** A modular, extensible simulation framework for network modeling.
- **OPNET (Riverbed Modeler):** A commercial tool for detailed network simulation and analysis.
- **GNS3:** A graphical network simulator that combines virtual and real devices.
- **MATLAB/Simulink:** A tool for simulating and analyzing network algorithms and systems.

Future Trends in Network Modeling

- **Integration with AI/ML:** Using machine learning to optimize network performance and predict traffic patterns.
- **5G and Beyond:** Modeling next-generation networks to support ultra-low latency and high-bandwidth applications.
- **Edge Computing:** Incorporating edge computing into network models to reduce latency and improve performance.
- **IoT Networks:** Modeling the unique challenges of IoT networks, such as scalability and energy efficiency.
- **Virtualization:** Simulating virtualized networks, including SDN (Software-Defined Networking) and NFV (Network Functions Virtualization).

4.2 SIMULATION METHODS FOR DESIGNING MULTIMEDIA NETWORKS

4.2.1 Introduction to Multimedia Networks

Multimedia networks are designed to support the transmission of various types of data, including audio, video, text, and images, often in real-time. These networks must meet strict Quality of Service (QoS) requirements, such as low latency, high bandwidth, and minimal packet loss. Simulation methods are essential for designing and optimizing multimedia networks, as they allow engineers to model and analyze network behavior under different conditions without the need for physical deployment.

4.2.2 Importance of Simulation in Multimedia Network Design

- **Cost-Effective:** Simulations reduce the need for expensive hardware and infrastructure during the design phase.
- **Risk Mitigation:** Engineers can test various scenarios, including failure conditions, without impacting a live network.

- **Performance Evaluation:** Simulations help in assessing the performance of the network under different traffic loads, protocols, and configurations.
- **Scalability Testing:** Simulations allow for testing the network's ability to handle increasing numbers of users or devices.

4.2.3 Key Components of Multimedia Network Simulation

- **Traffic Models:** Represent the behavior of multimedia traffic, such as video streaming, VoIP, or file transfers. Common models include Poisson, Markov, and self-similar traffic models.
- **Network Topology:** Defines the structure of the network, including nodes, links, and routing paths. Common topologies include star, mesh, and tree structures.
- **Protocols:** Simulate the behavior of network protocols (e.g., TCP/IP, UDP, RTP) to evaluate their impact on performance.
- **QoS Parameters:** Metrics such as delay, jitter, packet loss, and throughput are measured to ensure the network meets the required standards.
- **Resource Allocation:** Simulates how bandwidth, buffer space, and processing power are allocated to different types of traffic.

4.2.4 Simulation Tools for Multimedia Networks

- **NS-3 (Network Simulator 3):** An open-source tool widely used for simulating wired and wireless networks. It supports multimedia traffic and QoS parameters.
- **OMNeT++:** A modular, extensible simulation framework that supports detailed modeling of network protocols and multimedia applications.
- **OPNET (Riverbed Modeler):** A commercial tool that provides advanced features for simulating multimedia networks, including realistic traffic modeling and protocol analysis.
- **MATLAB/Simulink:** Useful for simulating and analyzing network algorithms, especially for signal processing and multimedia applications.
- **GNS3 (Graphical Network Simulator):** A tool that combines simulation with real devices, useful for testing multimedia applications in hybrid environments.

1. Steps in Multimedia Network Simulation

- **Define Objectives:** Identify the goals of the simulation, such as evaluating QoS, testing scalability, or optimizing resource allocation.
- **Model the Network:** Create a representation of the network topology, including nodes, links, and traffic sources.
- **Configure Parameters:** Set up traffic models, protocols, and QoS requirements based on the network's intended use.
- **Run the Simulation:** Execute the simulation under various conditions to collect data on network performance.
- **Analyze Results:** Evaluate the simulation output to identify bottlenecks, inefficiencies, or areas for improvement.
- **Iterate and Optimize:** Refine the network design based on simulation results and repeat the process until the desired performance is achieved.

2. Block Diagram Of Network Simulator Working

A block diagram of a Network Simulator typically includes the following components:

1. **User Interface**: Input for defining network topology, parameters, and simulation scenarios.
2. **Network Model**: Represents nodes, links, protocols, and devices.
3. **Event Scheduler**: Manages simulation events in chronological order.
4. **Protocol Stack**: Implements network protocols (e.g., TCP/IP, UDP).
5. **Traffic Generator**: Simulates data traffic and network load.
6. **Performance Analyzer**: Collects and analyzes simulation results (e.g., latency, throughput).
7. **Output/Visualization**: Displays results in graphs, logs, or animations.

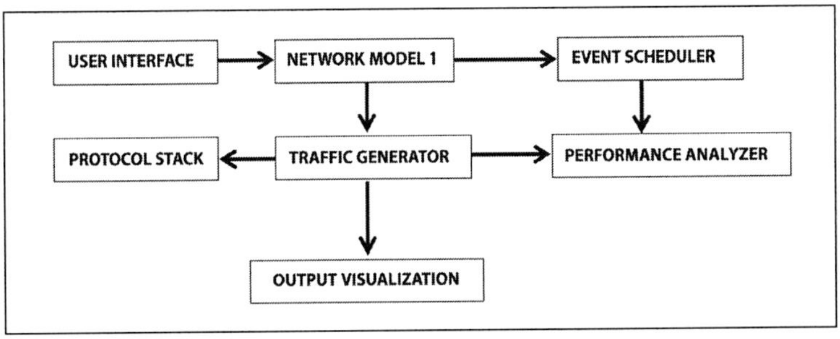

Fig. 4.3

4.2.5 Challenges in Multimedia Network Simulation

- **Complexity:** Multimedia traffic is highly variable and bursty, making it difficult to model accurately.
- **Real-Time Requirements:** Simulations must account for real-time constraints, such as low latency and synchronization.
- **Scalability:** Simulating large-scale networks with thousands of nodes can be computationally intensive.
- **Accuracy:** Ensuring that the simulation results closely match real-world behavior requires careful calibration of models and parameters.

4.2.6 Applications of Simulation In Multimedia Networks

- **Video Streaming:** Simulating video-on-demand services to optimize bandwidth usage and reduce buffering.
- **VoIP (Voice over IP):** Testing voice communication systems to ensure low latency and high call quality.
- **Online Gaming:** Evaluating network performance for real-time multiplayer games with strict latency requirements.
- **Teleconferencing:** Simulating video conferencing systems to ensure smooth communication and minimal delays.

4.2.7 Future Trends in Multimedia Network Simulation

- **Integration with AI/ML:** Using machine learning algorithms to optimize network performance and predict traffic patterns.
- **5G and Beyond**: Simulating next-generation networks to support ultra-low latency and high-bandwidth applications.
- **Edge Computing:** Modeling the impact of edge computing on multimedia networks to reduce latency and improve QoS.
- **Virtual Reality (VR) and Augmented Reality (AR):** Simulating networks to support immersive multimedia experiences with high data rates and low latency.

4.3 DETERMINING REMOTE BRIDGE AND ROUTER DELAYS

In computer networks, bridges and routers are critical devices that facilitate communication between different network segments. Understanding the delays introduced by these devices is essential for optimizing network performance, ensuring efficient data transmission, and diagnosing network issues. Remote bridge and router delays refer to the time taken for data packets to traverse these devices when communicating between distant networks.

4.3.1. Bridge Delays

- Bridges operate at the Data Link Layer (Layer 2) of the OSI model.
- They connect multiple network segments and forward frames based on MAC addresses.
- Delays in bridges are primarily caused by:
  - **Processing Delay:** Time taken to examine the frame's MAC address and make forwarding decisions.
  - **Queuing Delay:** Time frames spend waiting in buffers before being forwarded.
  - **Transmission Delay:** Time taken to transmit the frame onto the outgoing link.

4.3.2 Router Delays

- Routers operate at the Network Layer (Layer 3) of the OSI model.
- They connect different networks and forward packets based on IP addresses.
- Delays in routers are caused by:
  - **Processing Delay:** Time taken to process packet headers and determine the next hop.
  - **Queuing Delay:** Time packets spend in buffers waiting for transmission.
  - **Transmission Delay:** Time taken to push the packet onto the outgoing link.
  - **Propagation Delay:** Time taken for the packet to travel over the physical medium.

4.3.3 Factors Affecting Remote Bridge and Router Delays

1. Network Topology

Complex topologies with multiple bridges and routers increase delays due to additional hops.

2. Traffic Load

High traffic volumes can lead to congestion, increasing queuing and processing delays.

3. Device Performance

The processing power and efficiency of bridges and routers impact delays.

4. Link Bandwidth

Lower bandwidth links increase transmission delays.

5. Distance

Greater physical distances between devices increase propagation delays.

4.3.4 METHODS TO DETERMINE DELAYS

1. General Method

(i) Processing Delay ((D_processing))

- Time taken by a bridge or router to process a packet (e.g., examining headers, making forwarding decisions).

  D_processing = Time per packet
- **Example:**
- If a router takes 0.1 ms to process each packet, then: D_processing = 0.1 , ms

(ii) Queuing Delay ((D_queuing))

- Time a packet spends waiting in a buffer before being transmitted.
- Depends on traffic load and queue size.

  D_queuing = (Average queue length / Link bandwidth)
- **Example:**
- If the average queue length is 10 packets and the link bandwidth is 1 Mbps (125,000 bytes/sec):

  D_queuing = (10 *1500 bytes/125,000 bytes/sec)= 0.12 , seconds

(iii) Transmission Delay ((D_transmission))

- Time taken to push a packet onto the link.

  D_transmission = Packet size (bits)/Bandwidth (bps)
- **Example:**
- **If the packet size is 1500 bytes (12,000 bits) and the bandwidth is 1 Mbps (1,000,000 bps):**

  D_transmission = 12,000 bits/1,000,000 , bps = 0.012 , seconds

(iv) Propagation Delay ((D_propagation))

- Time taken for a packet to travel over the physical medium.

  D_propagation = Distance (meters)/Propagation speed (meters/sec)

- Propagation speed in fiber or copper is approximately (2 times 10^8 , m/s).
- **Example:**
- **If the distance between two devices is 100 km (100,000 meters):**
  D_propagation = 100,000 meters/2 * 10^8 m/s = 0.0005 , seconds

(v) Total Delay ((D_total))

- **The total delay ((D_total)) in a network is the sum of the following components:**
  D_total = D_processing + D_queuing + D_transmission + D_propagation
- Where:
  - (D_processing) = Processing delay
  - (D_queuing) = Queuing delay
  - (D_transmission) = Transmission delay
  - (D_propagation) = Propagation delay

Example Calculation of Total Delay

Scenario: A packet of size 1500 bytes is sent over a 1 Mbps link. The router has a processing delay of 0.1 ms. The average queuing delay is 0.12 seconds. The distance between the source and destination is 100 km.

Step 1: Calculate Transmission Delay

D_transmission = 12,000 bits/1000,000 bps = 0.012 , seconds

Step 2: Calculate Propagation Delay

D_propagation = 100,000 meters / 2 *10^8 , m/s = 0.0005 , seconds

Step 3: Add All Delays

D_total = D_processing + D_queuing + D_transmission + D_propagation

D_total = 0.0001 , seconds + 0.12 , seconds + 0.012 , seconds + 0.0005 , seconds

D_total = 0.1326 , seconds

2. Ping and Traceroute

- **Ping:** Measures round-trip time (RTT) between source and destination, providing an estimate of total delay.

Example:

- If the RTT is 50 ms, the one-way delay is approximately 25 ms.
- **Traceroute:** Identifies the path taken by packets and measures delays at each hop, helping isolate delays caused by specific bridges or routers.

Example:

Output :

- **Hop 1:** 10.0.0.1, Delay = 5 ms
- **Hop 2:** 192.168.1.1, Delay = 10 ms
- **Hop 3:** 203.0.113.1, Delay = 15 ms
- Total delay = (5 + 10 + 15 = 30 , ms).

3. Network Monitoring Tools

Tools like Wireshark, PRTG, or SolarWinds can capture and analyze network traffic to measure delays.

4. Simulation Tools

Network simulators like NS2, NS3, or GNS3 can model network behavior and estimate delays.

5. Hardware Diagnostics

Built-in diagnostic tools in bridges and routers can provide delay metrics.

4.3.5 Reducing Remote Bridge and Router Delays

1. Optimize Network Design

- Minimize the number of hops between source and destination.
- Use efficient routing protocols (e.g., OSPF, EIGRP).

2. Upgrade Hardware

- Use high-performance bridges and routers with faster processing capabilities.

3. Traffic Management

- Implement Quality of Service (QoS) to prioritize critical traffic and reduce queuing delays.

4. Increase Bandwidth

- Upgrade links to higher bandwidth to reduce transmission delays.

5. Regular Maintenance

- Monitor and troubleshoot network devices to ensure optimal performance.

4.4 NETWORK BASELINING AS A PLANNING TOOL

Network baselining is the process of measuring and documenting the performance and behavior of a network under normal operating conditions. It serves as a critical planning tool for network administrators, enabling them to establish a performance benchmark, identify trends, and make informed decisions about network upgrades, optimizations, and troubleshooting.

4.4.1 Purpose of Network Baselining

1. Performance Benchmarking

- Establishes a reference point for normal network performance.
- Helps in identifying deviations from expected behavior.

2. Capacity Planning

Provides data to predict future network requirements and plan for scalability.

3. Troubleshooting

Facilitates quick identification of performance bottlenecks or anomalies.

4. Optimization

Highlights areas for improvement, such as upgrading hardware or reconfiguring network settings.

5. Compliance and Reporting

Ensures the network meets performance standards and supports audit requirements.

4.4.2 STEPS IN NETWORK BASELINING

1. Define Objectives

Determine the purpose of the baseline (e.g., performance monitoring, capacity planning, troubleshooting).

2. Identify Key Metrics

Select metrics relevant to the network's performance, such as:

- **Bandwidth Utilization:** Percentage of available bandwidth being used.
- **Latency:** Time taken for data to travel from source to destination.
- **Packet Loss:** Percentage of packets lost during transmission.
- **Jitter:** Variation in packet arrival times.
- **Error Rates:** Number of transmission errors.

3. Select Tools

Use network monitoring and analysis tools to collect data, such as:

- **Wireshark:** For packet-level analysis.
- **PRTG Network Monitor:** For real-time monitoring.
- **SolarWinds Network Performance Monitor:** For comprehensive performance tracking.
- **Ping and Traceroute:** For basic latency and path analysis.

4. Collect Data

- Gather data over a specific period (e.g., days, weeks, or months) to capture normal network behaviour.
- Ensure data is collected during both peak and off-peak hours.

5. Analyze Data

- Compare collected data against predefined thresholds or historical trends.
- Identify patterns, anomalies, or areas of concern.

6. Document Findings

- Create a detailed report summarizing the baseline metrics, observations, and recommendations.

7. Implement Improvements

- Use the baseline data to optimize network performance, upgrade infrastructure, or resolve issues.

8. Regular Updates

- Periodically update the baseline to reflect changes in network usage, topology, or technology.

4.4.3 Benefits of Network Baselining

1. Proactive Management

Enables early detection of potential issues before they impact users.

2. Informed Decision-Making

Provides data-driven insights for planning upgrades or reconfigurations.

3. Improved Performance

Helps optimize network resources and reduce bottlenecks.

4. Cost Efficiency

Prevents unnecessary expenditures by identifying actual network needs.

5. Enhanced User Experience

Ensures consistent and reliable network performance for end-users.

4.4.4 Challenges in Network Baselining

1. Data Overload

Collecting and analyzing large volumes of data can be time-consuming.

2. Dynamic Environments

Networks are constantly evolving, making it challenging to maintain an up-to-date baseline.

3. Tool Limitations

Not all tools provide comprehensive insights, requiring a combination of solutions.

4. Resource Intensive

Requires skilled personnel and dedicated resources for effective implementation.

4.4.5 Best Practices for Network Baselining

1. Start Smal

Focus on critical network segments before expanding to the entire network.

2. Use Automated Tools

Leverage tools that automate data collection and analysis to save time.

3. Regular Updates

Periodically update the baseline to reflect changes in network usage and technology.

4. Collaborate with Stakeholders

Involve IT teams, management, and end-users to align baselining efforts with organizational goals.

5. Document Everything

Maintain detailed records of baseline metrics, analysis, and actions taken.

SUMMARY

- It gives a clear factors on contributing to delays and using appropriate tools and techniques, network administrators can diagnose issues, optimize network design, and ensure smooth data transmission across networks.
- Simulation methods are indispensable for designing and optimizing multimedia networks, enabling engineers to test and refine network designs in a controlled environment.

TEACHER'S KNOW MORE

- **Simulation for Multimedia Networks:** Use tools like NS2, NS3, or Packet Tracer to predict network performance and optimize multimedia traffic.
- **Remote Bridge & Router Delays:** Explain factors affecting delays, including congestion, processing time, and propagation.
- **Network Baselining:** Teach how to collect and analyze baseline data for performance monitoring and future planning.
- **Optimization Techniques:** Cover QoS, traffic engineering, and bandwidth management for efficient network performance.
- **Practical Learning:** Use real-world scenarios and hands-on simulations to reinforce network planning concepts.

EXERCISE

A. Subjective Questions

Category-I *(Revised Bloom's Level-1, 2 & 3)*

1. Define multimedia networking and its role in modern communication. *(Level 1 - Remembering)*
2. List the main components required to design a multimedia network. *(Level 1 - Remembering)*
3. Explain the importance of simulation methods in network design. *(Level 2 - Understanding)*
4. Describe how remote bridges and routers affect data transmission. *(Level 2 - Understanding)*
5. Illustrate a simple multimedia network topology with labeled components. *(Level 3 - Applying)*

6. Compare the functions of a router and a bridge in a multimedia network. *(Level 3 - Applying)*

7. Summarize the challenges of real-time multimedia transmission over a network. *(Level 2 - Understanding)*

8. Identify key performance metrics used to measure network efficiency. *(Level 1 - Remembering)*

9. Discuss the impact of network congestion on multimedia streaming quality. *(Level 2 - Understanding)*

10. Demonstrate how network baselining helps in capacity planning. *(Level 3 - Applying)*

Category-II ***(Revised Bloom's Level-4, 5 & 6)***

1. Analyze the role of simulation techniques in optimizing multimedia network performance. *(Level 4 - Analyzing)*
2. Differentiate between remote bridge delay and router delay. *(Level 4 - Analyzing)*
3. Evaluate the impact of increased latency on video conferencing and online gaming. *(Level 5 - Evaluating)*
4. Assess the benefits of network baselining in performance monitoring. *(Level 5 - Evaluating)*
5. Examine the reasons why packet loss occurs in multimedia networks. *(Level 4 - Analyzing)*
6. Critique the effectiveness of Quality of Service (QoS) mechanisms in minimizing delay. *(Level 5 - Evaluating)*
7. Propose a simulation model to predict and reduce network congestion. *(Level 6 - Creating)*
8. Design a multimedia network that ensures minimal delay and high efficiency. *(Level 6 - Creating)*
9. Develop a strategy for optimizing router placement in a large-scale multimedia network. *(Level 6 - Creating)*
10. Construct a method to automate network baselining for dynamic environments. *(Level 6 - Creating)*

B. Objective Questions

Category-I ***(Revised Bloom's Level-1, 2 & 3)***

1. Which of the following is NOT a key component of a multimedia network? *(Level 1 - Remembering)*

   (a) Router (b) Bridge

   (c) Speaker (d) Switch

2. What is the primary purpose of network simulation? *(Level 2 - Understanding)*

   (a) To increase internet speed

   (b) To analyze and predict network performance

   (c) To replace physical hardware

   (d) To create multimedia content

3. How does a remote bridge affect network performance? *(Level 2 - Understanding)*
   (a) It reduces latency (b) It causes data loss
   (c) It introduces delay (d) It improves video streaming
4. Which factor is most responsible for delays in routers? *(Level 3 - Applying)*
   (a) High processing time (b) Lack of internet connection
   (c) High number of physical ports (d) Wireless interference
5. What does network baselining primarily help with? *(Level 2 - Understanding)*
   (a) Security threat detection
   (b) Performance monitoring and planning
   (c) Increasing bandwidth
   (d) Reducing hardware costs
6. Which of the following techniques reduces router delay in multimedia networks? *(Level 3 - Applying)*
   (a) Increasing queue size (b) Reducing packet size
   (c) Using a slower routing algorithm (d) Adding more firewalls
7. What is the most common cause of jitter in multimedia communication? *(Level 2 - Understanding)*
   (a) Packet loss (b) High-speed internet
   (c) Fiber-optic networks (d) Low latency
8. What is a major drawback of not conducting network baselining? *(Level 3 - Applying)*
   (a) Increased operational costs (b) No impact on network performance
   (c) Improved latency (d) Higher bandwidth availability
9. How can a network administrator improve bridge efficiency? *(Level 3 - Applying)*
   (a) Reduce the number of VLANs (b) Increase the number of switches
   (c) Implement load balancing (d) Remove encryption
10. Which network component is most critical for reducing latency in multimedia networks? *(Level 2 - Understanding)*
   (a) Router (b) Firewall
   (c) Hub (d) Repeater

Ans.: 1. (c), 2. (b), 3. (c), 4. (a), 5. (b), 6. (b), 7. (a), 8. (a), 9. (c), 10. (a)

Category-II ***(Revised Bloom's Level-4, 5 & 6)***

1. What is the best strategy to minimize remote bridge delays? *(Level 4 - Analyzing)*
   (a) Increase network redundancy (b) Use slower links
   (c) Implement static routing (d) Remove firewalls
2. Which factor most influences multimedia transmission efficiency? *(Level 4 - Analyzing)*
   (a) CPU speed of the server (b) Network topology and routing protocol
   (c) File size of multimedia content (d) Antivirus software

3. What is the most effective way to reduce buffering in video streaming? *(Level 5 - Evaluating)*
   (a) Increase bandwidth (b) Reduce video resolution
   (c) Optimize network congestion control (d) Install more firewalls
4. A network engineer wants to evaluate router performance. Which metric should they prioritize? *(Level 5 - Evaluating)*
   (a) Link utilization (b) MAC address count
   (c) Packet forwarding delay (d) Device model number
5. How can a network administrator optimize network baselining? *(Level 5 - Evaluating)*
   (a) By manually checking network logs
   (b) By automating performance data collection
   (c) By ignoring normal traffic fluctuations
   (d) By disabling QoS policies
6. What is the best method to ensure minimal latency in a multimedia network? *(Level 6 - Creating)*
   (a) Design a high-speed backbone (b) Add multiple firewalls
   (c) Use a single network switch (d) Increase buffer size in routers
7. Which method is most effective in reducing router queuing delays? *(Level 6 - Creating)*
   (a) Implementing QoS (b) Increasing packet loss
   (c) Using lower bandwidth (d) Disabling caching
8. What innovative method can improve real-time video streaming performance? *(Level 6 - Creating)*
   (a) AI-based traffic optimization (b) Slower packet processing
   (c) Increased firewall rules (d) Manual bandwidth management
9. What is the primary goal of network planning in multimedia networks?
   (a) To maximize latency
   (b) To ensure reliable and high-quality service delivery
   (c) To reduce the number of connected devices
   (d) To eliminate the need for simulation
10. Which of the following is a limitation of network simulation tools?
   (a) They cannot model real-world network conditions accurately
   (b) They are too expensive to use
   (c) They require no computational resources
   (d) They are only useful for small networks

Ans.: 1. (a), 2. (b), 3. (c), 4. (c), 5. (b), 6. (a), 7. (a), 8. (a), 9. (b), 10. (a)

This page is intentionally left blank!

5

UNIT

Evolving Technologies

RATIONALE

This unit explores modern broadband and communication technologies, focusing on xDSL and cable modems for high-speed internet access. It examines voice and video integration on LANs, the role of Internet voice applications, and the implementation of IP PBX telephony networks. It covers Fax over IP (FoIP) and videoconferencing over IP networks, highlighting their advantages in cost reduction, scalability, and efficiency. The unit equips learners with the skills to design and optimize IP-based communication solutions for seamless connectivity.

OUTCOMES

- Evaluate Broadband and Communication Technologies:
- Assess the merits of xDSL and cable modem technologies for high-speed internet access, and analyze their impact on voice and video transmission over LANs.
- Implement and Optimize IP-based Communication Solutions:
- Design and configure IP PBX telephony networks, Fax over IP, and videoconferencing systems to enhance communication efficiency and ensure seamless integration of internet voice applications.

5.1 TRENDS IN DATA COMMUNICATIONS

These trends reflect the ongoing transformation in data communication technologies and point toward a future where networks are faster, more flexible, and capable of handling more complex and diverse demands. Some of the current key trends in the field:

5G Networks

The rollout of 5G networks is revolutionizing data communications by offering ultra-fast speeds, low latency, and the ability to connect millions of devices. 5G networks are expected to support a wide range of applications, including autonomous vehicles, smart cities, and the Internet of Things (IoT). Looking ahead, research into 6G is already underway, aiming to provide even faster speeds, higher reliability, and more intelligent network management.

Edge Computing

Edge computing is becoming more popular as it reduces the reliance on centralized data centers by processing data closer to the source, which minimizes latency and bandwidth usage. This is especially important for real-time applications, such as video streaming, online gaming, and industrial automation, where immediate processing and decision-making are critical.

Artificial Intelligence (AI) in Networking

AI and machine learning are increasingly being integrated into data communications to improve network management, security, and performance. AI-driven tools can optimize traffic routing, predict and prevent network failures, and enhance cybersecurity by detecting anomalies and threats in real time.

Software-Defined Networking (SDN)

SDN continues to transform how data networks are designed and managed by decoupling the control plane from the data plane. This allows for more flexibility and easier configuration of networks, enabling dynamic adjustment based on traffic demands and reducing the complexity of network management.

Network Function Virtualization (NFV)

NFV enables the virtualization of network services like firewalls, load balancers, and routers. This reduces the need for specialized hardware and allows for faster deployment and scaling of services. It supports the trend toward more agile, cost-effective, and scalable networking infrastructure.

Quantum Computing and Communication

Although still in the early stages, quantum computing is expected to revolutionize data communication by enabling ultra-fast processing speeds. Quantum communication, particularly quantum key distribution (QKD), is being explored for its potential to offer secure communication channels, as it is theoretically immune to eavesdropping.

The Rise of the Internet of Things (IoT)

The proliferation of IoT devices continues to drive growth in data communications. With billions of connected devices generating vast amounts of data, networks must evolve to handle increased traffic, integrate various communication protocols, and ensure security for IoT environments.

Cybersecurity and Privacy Concerns

As more sensitive data is transmitted across networks, cybersecurity and privacy are top priorities. Data encryption, secure communication protocols, and advanced threat detection methods are essential to protecting data integrity. Additionally, new regulations like GDPR and CCPA are pushing organizations to adopt better data protection practices.

Wi-Fi 6 and Wi-Fi 6E

Wi-Fi 6 (also known as 802.11ax) and the newer Wi-Fi 6E standard, which operates in the 6 GHz spectrum, are designed to improve wireless communication by offering faster speeds, higher capacity, and better performance in crowded environments. These advancements are important for both consumer and enterprise applications, including high-bandwidth activities like video conferencing and virtual reality.

Cloud-Native Networking

With the rise of cloud computing, cloud-native technologies such as containerization and microservices are increasingly influencing data communication architectures. Cloud-native networking enables more efficient communication between distributed systems, supports scalability, and simplifies the management of network infrastructure in multi-cloud environments.

5.2 MERITS OF XDSL TECHNOLOGY

xDSL (Digital Subscriber Line) technologies, including ADSL (Asymmetric DSL), SDSL (Symmetric DSL), and VDSL (Very High-Speed DSL), provide high-speed data transmission over existing copper telephone lines. The merits of xDSL technologies include:

Cost-Effective

Since xDSL uses the existing telephone infrastructure, there is no need for expensive new wiring, making it a cost-effective solution for both service providers and end-users. For example, a home user can access high-speed internet without the need for fiber-optic connections.

High-Speed Data Transmission

xDSL technologies offer faster speeds compared to traditional dial-up connections. ADSL, for instance, can deliver speeds of up to 24 Mbps downstream and 1 Mbps upstream, making it suitable for internet browsing, streaming, and light business applications.

Simultaneous Voice and Data Transmission

xDSL can support simultaneous voice and data services over the same line. This is beneficial for businesses and residential users who need to make voice calls while using the internet. For example, a person can be on a VoIP (Voice over IP) call while browsing the internet without any interference.

Availability and Reach

xDSL can be deployed over long distances, as the technology can be used in areas where fiber-optic networks are not feasible due to cost or infrastructure limitations. This makes it widely accessible, even in rural or remote areas.

Scalability

xDSL networks are scalable, meaning that they can be upgraded as demand for bandwidth increases. VDSL, for example, offers significantly higher speeds and can cater to more intensive applications like HD video streaming and online gaming.

Low Latency

xDSL technology generally offers low latency, which is critical for applications like video conferencing and online gaming where delays can be disruptive.

5.3 PREPARING FOR CABLE MODEMS

Cable modems utilize coaxial cables, traditionally used for cable television, to deliver high-speed internet access. Proper preparation involves upgrading infrastructure, ensuring compatibility with existing services, improving signal transmission, and enhancing security measures.

Infrastructure Upgrades

Modern internet applications, such as 4K video streaming, online gaming, and cloud computing, require substantial bandwidth. To meet these demands, cable networks must undergo upgrades to enhance both upstream and downstream data transmission.

Example: In the United States, major providers like Comcast have upgraded their networks with fiber-optic backbones to support faster cable internet speeds, allowing for better performance in high-demand areas.

Integration with Existing Services

Cable modems must be compatible with television and VoIP phone services to ensure a seamless user experience. Many ISPs bundle services, requiring efficient frequency allocation to prevent signal interference.

Example: Companies like Spectrum offer bundled packages that include cable TV, internet, and phone services. Their modems are designed to handle multiple services without causing disruptions in voice calls or TV broadcasts.

Advanced Signal Transmission Technologies

Cable modems use **DOCSIS (Data Over Cable Service Interface Specification)** to regulate data transfer over coaxial cables. Upgrading to DOCSIS 3.0 or 3.1 enhances internet speeds, reduces latency, and improves network management.

Example: A household using a DOCSIS 2.0 modem might experience slower speeds and buffering while streaming Netflix in 4K. Upgrading to a DOCSIS 3.1 modem can provide gigabit speeds, ensuring smooth streaming without interruptions.

Security Measures and Threat Prevention

Faster internet speeds also bring an increased risk of cyber threats, making strong security measures essential. This includes encryption, firewalls, and regular firmware updates.

Example: In 2019, a major cyberattack targeted unprotected home routers and modems, allowing hackers to access sensitive user data. ISPs like AT&T and Verizon responded by improving encryption standards and pushing security updates to prevent such breaches.

5.4 VOICE AND VIDEO ON THE LAN (LOCAL AREA NETWORK)

Voice and video over the LAN refers to the use of a network to carry voice and video signals, rather than relying on traditional telephone or television services.

VoIP (Voice over IP)

VoIP allows voice communication over the internet or a private LAN. Using protocols like SIP (Session Initiation Protocol), voice can be transmitted as data packets over the network, enabling lower-cost communication, especially for long-distance calls. **For example** a small business uses a VoIP system like **RingCentral** or **Vonage** to handle both internal and external communications. The company has remote employees across different locations, and by utilizing VoIP, they can make voice calls over the internet instead of relying on traditional phone lines. This significantly reduces their monthly phone bill, especially for long-distance calls. When a customer calls, they are greeted by an automated system, which then directs them to the appropriate employee based on their need. The business also benefits from additional features like voicemail-to-email, call forwarding, and conferencing, all managed through a simple web interface. In this scenario, the company benefits from the **SIP (Session Initiation Protocol)** used by VoIP systems to manage voice call connections, allowing easy communication between remote employees and clients using just an internet connection.

5.5 IP VIDEO CONFERENCING

Video conferencing over a LAN uses protocols like H.264 and WebRTC (Web Real-Time Communication) to provide high-quality video and audio communication over the network. This is essential for businesses and educational institutions that need to collaborate remotely.

For example a university is conducting online classes and uses **Zoom** for video conferencing with its students. The platform relies on **WebRTC (Web Real-Time Communication)** to ensure real-time video and audio communication between the instructors and students, regardless of their location. In addition to video and audio, the platform also supports features like screen sharing, real-time chat, and digital white boarding, all of which enhance the remote learning experience. The video quality is high due to the **H.264** video compression standard, which optimizes bandwidth usage while maintaining good video clarity. This is especially important since students may join the conference from various locations, some of which might have limited internet speeds. For the university, the flexibility of IP video conferencing saves on travel costs and allows for efficient collaboration without the need for physical presence.

Cost-Effective Communication

Using the LAN for voice and video eliminates the need for separate communication systems. This reduces hardware and maintenance costs for businesses.

Example: A company uses a VoIP solution like Zoom or Microsoft Teams for voice and video calls within the organization, all running over the company's internal LAN.

5.6 INTERNET VOICE APPLICATIONS

Internet voice applications enable voice communication over the internet using various technologies like VoIP, SIP, or WebRTC.

VoIP Services

Services like Skype, WhatsApp, and Google Voice allow users to make voice calls over the internet. These services are cost-effective, as they bypass traditional telephony systems, especially for international calls.

Web-Based Voice Calling

WebRTC enables voice calling directly from browsers without requiring plugins or additional software. This is often used in customer service applications or on websites offering live chat with voice support.

Enhanced Features

Internet voice applications may offer features like voicemail, call forwarding, conference calling, and integration with other applications (e.g., CRM software).

Example: A small business uses a VoIP service like RingCentral to handle both internal and external calls over the internet, providing better scalability and lower communication costs.

5.7 BUILDING AN IP PBX TELEPHONY NETWORK

An **IP PBX (Internet Protocol Private Branch Exchange)** is a modern telephony system that facilitates voice communication over an IP network, replacing conventional landline-based PBX systems. By utilizing **Voice over IP (VoIP)** technology, IP PBX enables organizations to manage internal and external calls efficiently while reducing infrastructure costs. Unlike traditional phone systems that require dedicated copper wiring, IP PBX systems operate over existing data networks, making them a cost-effective and scalable solution for businesses.

Cost Savings

One of the primary advantages of an IP PBX system is its affordability compared to traditional telephony networks. Since it operates over an organization's existing **internet and local area network (LAN)**, there is no need to install separate telephone lines. This significantly lowers initial setup expenses and ongoing maintenance costs. Additionally, VoIP calls, especially for long-distance and international communication, are much cheaper than calls made over conventional public switched telephone networks (PSTN). Many businesses also benefit from **reduced hardware requirements**, as softphones (software-based phones) can be used on computers and mobile devices instead of purchasing dedicated desk phones.For example, a company transitioning from a traditional PBX to an IP PBX can use its existing internet connection to handle voice communication, eliminating the need for expensive phone line rentals and reducing telecommunication expenses.

Flexibility and Scalability

IP PBX systems offer a high degree of flexibility and scalability, making them suitable for businesses of all sizes. Expanding a traditional PBX system often requires additional wiring, hardware, and physical installations, which can be costly and time-consuming. In contrast, an IP PBX allows for easy expansion through software-based configurations. Adding new users, extensions, or features can be done remotely through a web-based control panel, without the need for extensive technical modifications. The advanced call management features, such as voicemail, call forwarding, call recording, and automated attendants, can be configured effortlessly. Conference calling and integration with mobile devices further enhance communication, ensuring employees remain connected regardless of their location.For example, a rapidly growing business can increase its workforce and add more phone lines without needing to install additional hardware—simply by modifying software settings within the IP PBX system.

Integration with Other Systems

A major benefit of IP PBX technology is its ability to integrate with various business communication tools and software applications. Many IP PBX solutions are designed to work seamlessly with Customer Relationship Management (CRM) systems, email clients, and team collaboration platforms. This enables organizations to streamline workflows and enhance productivity.

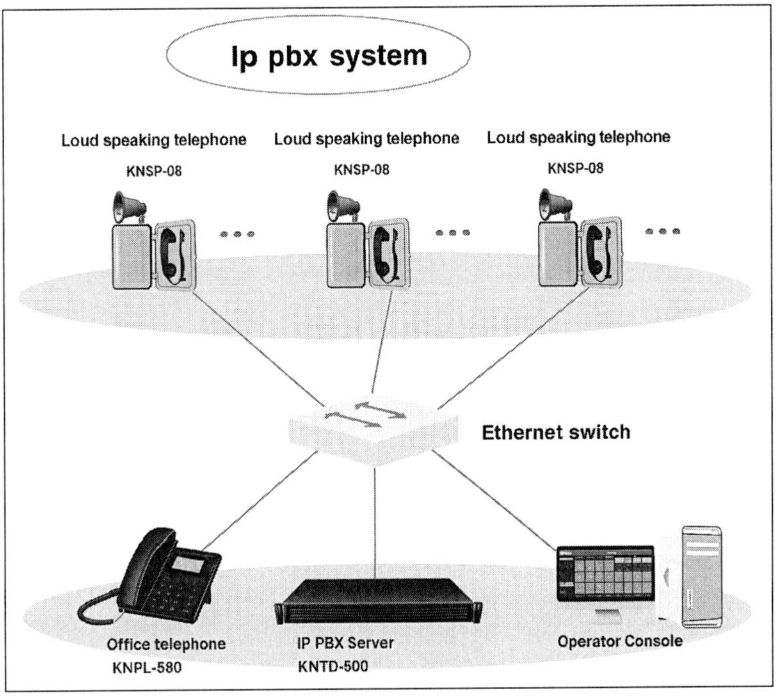

Fig. 5.1: IP PBX system

For instance, a company using an IP PBX system like Asterisk or FreePBX can link it with their CRM software to log customer interactions, automate call routing based on customer inquiries, and provide personalized service. Integration with email services allows voicemail-to-email functionality, where voicemails are automatically converted into audio files and sent directly to users' inboxes for easy access.Example: A corporate office implements an Asterisk-based IP PBX to enable employees to make and receive calls using their desktop computers, mobile phones, or VoIP desk phones. The system is also linked to their Microsoft Teams workspace, allowing seamless internal communication and video conferencing without requiring a separate platform.

5.8 FAX OVER IP (FOIP)

Traditional faxing requires dedicated analog phone lines, making it costly and inefficient. Fax over IP (FoIP) is a modern alternative that allows faxes to be sent and received over the internet using protocols like T.38, eliminating the need for physical phone lines. This transition helps organizations modernize their document transmission processes while reducing operational expenses.

Cost Efficiency

FoIP eliminates the dependency on analog phone lines specifically for faxing, leading to significant cost savings. Businesses that previously needed multiple fax machines with separate telephone connections can now consolidate all faxing operations into a single IP-based system. Additionally, FoIP reduces the need for paper, ink, and maintenance costs associated with traditional fax machines, making it a more sustainable option.

For example, a law firm that frequently exchanges legal documents via fax can switch to a cloud-based FoIP service, reducing expenses related to maintaining dedicated phone lines for faxing.

Faster Transmission

Unlike traditional faxing, which transmits data over analog phone lines at relatively slow speeds, FoIP leverages high-speed internet connections to send faxes quickly and reliably. This results in shorter transmission times, fewer transmission errors, and improved reliability. Additionally, FoIP supports real-time error correction, ensuring that faxed documents reach their recipients intact without issues like distorted text or missing pages. For instance, a healthcare provider using FoIP to send patient records between different branches can experience faster delivery times, ensuring timely access to critical documents.

Integration with Modern Systems

One of the key advantages of FoIP is its ability to integrate with digital document workflows. Instead of requiring a dedicated fax machine, users can send and receive faxes directly from their email accounts, cloud storage services, or office management systems. This enhances accessibility, allowing faxes to be securely stored, searched, and retrieved whenever needed. Many organizations also use electronic signatures and document automation tools to further streamline their faxing processes. For example, a business that uses Google Drive or Microsoft OneDrive can automatically save incoming faxes as PDFs in a designated cloud folder, making document management more efficient and environmentally friendly.

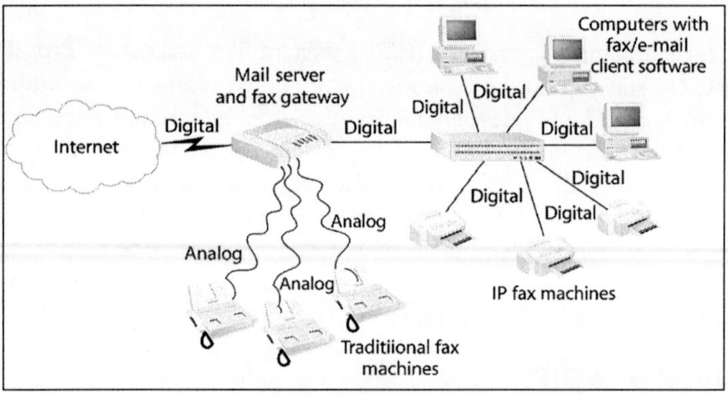

Fig. 5.2: Fax Over IP (FoIP)

The above figure illustrates a Fax over IP (FoIP) system using the ITU T.37 standard. It connects traditional analog fax machines and digital IP fax machines through a mail server and fax gateway. Computers with fax or email client software also integrate into the network for digital communication. The internet enables fax transmission, replacing conventional phone lines with IP-based solutions.

5.9 VIDEO CONFERENCING OVER IP NETWORKS

Video conferencing over IP networks enables real-time audio and video communication across the internet, allowing individuals and businesses to connect seamlessly. With advancements in broadband technology and efficient data compression, video conferencing has become an essential tool for remote collaboration, education, and corporate meetings.

Global Connectivity

One of the biggest advantages of video conferencing over IP is the ability to connect with participants from anywhere in the world. This eliminates geographical barriers, reducing travel costs and increasing productivity. Whether for business meetings, virtual training sessions, or remote learning, IP-based video conferencing ensures seamless interaction across different time zones.

Example: A multinational company can hold regular virtual meetings with teams across different countries, reducing travel expenses and enhancing operational efficiency.

High-Quality Communication

Modern video compression technologies, such as **H.264, H.265 (HEVC), and VP9**, enable high-definition video and clear audio transmission, even over bandwidth-constrained networks. Adaptive bitrate streaming ensures smooth video playback by adjusting quality based on network conditions. Noise reduction and echo cancellation technologies further improve audio clarity, making virtual conversations feel more natural.

Example: Telemedicine services rely on high-quality video and audio to allow doctors to diagnose and consult patients remotely, ensuring effective virtual healthcare.

Collaboration Tools for Enhanced Productivity

Most video conferencing platforms integrate advanced collaboration features, including:

- **Screen sharing** for presentations and demonstrations
- **File sharing** to distribute documents instantly
- **Virtual whiteboards** for brainstorming sessions
- **Chat and reactions** for real-time engagement without interrupting speakers

Example: A project team working remotely can use Microsoft Teams to share project updates, discuss reports via chat, and collaborate on documents in real time.

Security and Reliability

As video conferencing becomes more widespread, securing communication is crucial. Encryption protocols like **TLS (Transport Layer Security) and AES (Advanced Encryption Standard)** help protect sensitive information from cyber threats. Authentication methods, such as multi-factor authentication (MFA), ensure only authorized users access meetings.

Example: Financial institutions conducting virtual board meetings use end-to-end encrypted platforms like Cisco Webex to ensure confidentiality and compliance with data protection regulations.

SUMMARY

This unit explores emerging trends in data communications, focusing on xDSL technology and cable modems for high-speed internet access. It examines the integration of voice and video on LANs, the role of Internet voice applications, and the implementation of IP PBX telephony networks for efficient communication. Additionally, it covers Fax over IP (FoIP) and videoconferencing over IP networks, highlighting their benefits in cost reduction, scalability, and improved collaboration in modern networking environments.

TEACHER'S KNOW MORE

- **Data Communication Trends:** Cover the evolution of broadband, fiber optics, 5G, and cloud-based networking.
- **xDSL & Cable Modems:** Explain their merits, speed, reliability, and role in high-speed internet access.
- **Voice & Video on LANs:** Discuss VoIP, QoS, and network optimization for seamless communication.
- **IP PBX & Internet Voice Applications:** Teach IP telephony, VoIP security, and enterprise PBX deployment.
- **Fax over IP & Videoconferencing:** Explore FoIP, video conferencing tools, and best practices for implementation.
- Hands-on labs using **network simulation tools** (e.g., Cisco Packet Tracer, GNS3)

EXERCISE

A. Subjective Questions

Category-I ***(Revised Bloom's Level-1, 2 & 3)***

1. Define data communication and explain its significance in modern networking. *(Level 1 - Remembering)*
2. List the major trends in data communications. *(Level 1 - Remembering)*
3. Explain the working principles of xDSL technology. *(Level 2 - Understanding)*
4. Describe the advantages of using cable modems for high-speed internet access. *(Level 2 - Understanding)*
5. Illustrate how Voice over IP (VoIP) functions within a LAN environment. *(Level 3 - Applying)*
6. Compare traditional telephony systems with IP PBX telephony networks. *(Level 3 - Applying)*
7. Summarize the role of Internet voice applications in modern communication. *(Level 2 - Understanding)*
8. Identify the key challenges of implementing videoconferencing over IP networks. *(Level 1 - Remembering)*
9. Discuss the benefits of using Fax over IP (FoIP) compared to traditional fax systems. *(Level 2 - Understanding)*
10. Demonstrate how Quality of Service (QoS) can enhance video and voice performance on a LAN. *(Level 3 - Applying)*

Category-II ***(Revised Bloom's Level-4, 5 & 6)***

1. Analyze the role of simulation techniques in optimizing multimedia network performance. *(Level 4 - Analyzing)*
2. Differentiate between remote bridge delay and router delay. *(Level 4 - Analyzing)*
3. Evaluate the impact of increased latency on video conferencing and online gaming. *(Level 5 - Evaluating)*

4. Assess the benefits of network baselining in performance monitoring. *(Level 5 - Evaluating)*

5. Examine the reasons why packet loss occurs in multimedia networks. *(Level 4 - Analyzing)*

6. Critique the effectiveness of Quality of Service (QoS) mechanisms in minimizing delay. *(Level 5 - Evaluating)*

7. Propose a simulation model to predict and reduce network congestion. *(Level 6 - Creating)*

8. Design a multimedia network that ensures minimal delay and high efficiency. *(Level 6 - Creating)*

9. Develop a strategy for optimizing router placement in a large-scale multimedia network. *(Level 6 - Creating)*

10. Construct a method to automate network baselining for dynamic environments. *(Level 6 - Creating)*

B. Objective Questions

Category-I (Revised Bloom's Level-1, 2 & 3

1. Which of the following is NOT a key component of a multimedia network? *(Level 1 - Remembering)*

   (a) Router (b) Bridge
   (c) Speaker (d) Switch

2. What is the primary purpose of network simulation? *(Level 2 - Understanding)*

   (a) To increase internet speed
   (b) To analyze and predict network performance
   (c) To replace physical hardware
   (d) To create multimedia content

3. How does a remote bridge affect network performance? *(Level 2 - Understanding)*

   (a) It reduces latency (b) It causes data loss
   (c) It introduces delay (d) It improves video streaming

4. Which factor is most responsible for delays in routers? *(Level 3 - Applying)*

   (a) High processing time (b) Lack of internet connection
   (c) High number of physical ports (d) Wireless interference

5. What does network baselining primarily help with? *(Level 2 - Understanding)*

   (a) Security threat detection
   (b) Performance monitoring and planning
   (c) Increasing bandwidth
   (d) Reducing hardware costs

6. Which of the following techniques reduces router delay in multimedia networks? *(Level 3 - Applying)*

   (a) Increasing queue size (b) Reducing packet size
   (c) Using a slower routing algorithm (d) Adding more firewalls

7. What is the most common cause of jitter in multimedia communication? *(Level 2 - Understanding)*
   (a) Packet loss (b) High-speed internet
   (c) Fiber-optic networks (d) Low latency
8. What is a major drawback of not conducting network baselining? *(Level 3 - Applying)*
   (a) Increased operational costs
   (b) No impact on network performance
   (c) Improved latency
   (d) Higher bandwidth availability
9. How can a network administrator improve bridge efficiency? *(Level 3 - Applying)*
   (a) Reduce the number of VLANs (b) Increase the number of switches
   (c) Implement load balancing (d) Remove encryption
10. Which network component is most critical for reducing latency in multimedia networks? *(Level 2 - Understanding)*
   (a) Router (b) Firewall
   (c) Hub (d) Repeater

Ans.: 1. (c), 2. (b), 3. (c), 4. (a), 5. (b), 6. (b), 7. (a), 8. (a), 9. (c), 10. (a)

Category-II *(Revised Bloom's Level-4, 5 & 6)*

1. What is the best strategy to minimize remote bridge delays? *(Level 4 - Analyzing)*
   (a) Increase network redundancy (b) Use slower links
   (c) Implement static routing (d) Remove firewalls
2. Which factor most influences multimedia transmission efficiency? *(Level 4 - Analyzing)*
   (a) CPU speed of the server
   (b) Network topology and routing protocol
   (c) File size of multimedia content
   (d) Antivirus software
3. What is the most effective way to reduce buffering in video streaming? *(Level 5 - Evaluating)*
   (a) Increase bandwidth (b) Reduce video resolution
   (c) Optimize network congestion control (d) Install more firewalls
4. A network engineer wants to evaluate router performance. Which metric should they prioritize? *(Level 5 - Evaluating)*
   (a) Link utilization (b) MAC address count
   (c) Packet forwarding delay (d) Device model number
5. How can a network administrator optimize network baselining? *(Level 5 - Evaluating)*
   (a) By manually checking network logs
   (b) By automating performance data collection

(c) By ignoring normal traffic fluctuations

(d) By disabling QoS policies

6. What is the best method to ensure minimal latency in a multimedia network? *(Level 6 - Creating)*

(a) Design a high-speed backbone (b) Add multiple firewalls

(c) Use a single network switch (d) Increase buffer size in routers

7. Which method is most effective in reducing router queuing delays? *(Level 6 - Creating)*

(a) Implementing QoS (b) Increasing packet loss

(c) Using lower bandwidth (d) Disabling caching

8. What innovative method can improve real-time video streaming performance? *(Level 6 - Creating)*

(a) AI-based traffic optimization (b) Slower packet processing

(c) Increased firewall rules (d) Manual bandwidth management

9. How can machine learning assist in network baselining? *(Level 6 - Creating)*

(a) By increasing manual intervention in network management

(b) By predicting future traffic patterns and automating optimization strategies

(c) By eliminating the need for network security protocols

(d) By reducing the number of network devices required

10. What is the future scope of simulation methods in network planning? *(Level 6 - Creating)*

(a) Limited to physical network infrastructure only

(b) Integration of AI, automation, and real-time analytics for predictive optimization

(c) Replacement of all hardware components in a network

(d) Reducing the need for internet-based communication

Ans.: 1. (a), 2. (b), 3. (c), 4. (c), 5. (b), 6. (a), 7. (a), 8. (a), 9. (b), 10. (b)

This page is intentionally left blank!